UNDERSTANDING THE DUAL ASPECTS OF
FAITH

MICHAEL SCANTLEBURY

UNDERSTANDING THE DUAL ASPECTS OF FAITH: AN IN-DEPTH STUDY
Copyright © 2023 by Michael Scantlebury

Editorial Consultant: Anita Thompson – 604-521-6042
Question Section: Anoja Wijesuriya – 604-314-6605

All rights reserved. Neither this publication nor any part of this publication may be reproduced or transmitted in any form or by any means, electronic or mechanical, including photocopying, recording or any information storage and retrieval system, without permission in writing from the author.

All Scripture quotations, unless otherwise indicated, are taken from the Revised Standard Version. Copyright © 1946, 1952, and 1971 the Division of Christian Education of the National Council of the Churches of Christ in the United States of America. Used by permission. All rights reserved. All Scriptures marked KJV are taken from the King James Version; all marked NIV are from The New International Version; and those marked MSG are from The Message Bible and is used by permission.

Hebrew and Greek definitions are from James Strong, Strong's Exhaustive Concordance of the Bible (Peabody, MA: Hendrickson Publishers, n.d.).

Michael Scantlebury has taken author's prerogative in capitalizing certain words that are not usually capitalized according to standard grammatical practice. Also, please note that the name satan and related names are not capitalized as we choose not to acknowledge him, even to the point of disregarding standard grammatical practice.

ISBN: 978-1-4866-2412-6
eBook ISBN: 978-1-4866-2413-3

Word Alive Press
119 De Baets Street Winnipeg, MB R2J 3R9
www.wordalivepress.ca

Cataloguing in Publication information is can be obtained from Library and Archives Canada.

BOOKS BY MICHAEL SCANTLEBURY

Understanding the Revelation
Are We Living in the End-Times or Last Days?
Heaven and Earth – A Biblical Understanding
Understanding the Kingdom of God and The Church of Jesus Christ
Eschatology – A Biblical View
As It Was in the Beginning, So Shall It Be...
Daniel In Babylon – The Study Guide
Principles for Victorious Living Volume II
Principles for Victorious Living Volume I
Present Truth Lifestyle – Daniel In Babylon
Esther: Present Truth Church
The Fortress Church
Called to be An Apostle – An Autobiography
Leaven Revealed
Five Pillars of The Apostolic
Apostolic Purity
Apostolic Reformation
Jesus Christ The Apostle and High Priest of Our Profession
Kingdom Advancing Prayer Volume I
Kingdom Advancing Prayer Volume II
Kingdom Advancing Prayer Volume III
Internal Reformation
God's Nature Expressed Through His Names
"I Will Build My Church." – Jesus Christ
Identifying and Defeating the Jezebel Spirit

Contents

Foreword	VII
Introduction	IX
Chapter One **Faith – What Is It?**	1
Chapter Two **Some Things About Faith**	15
Chapter Three **How Can We Increase Our Faith?**	23
Chapter Four **Faith to Obtain**	29
Chapter Five **Nothing Changes Until You Change It By Faith In Jesus**	33
Chapter Six **Heroes of Faith**	37
Chapter Seven **Another Look at Faith**	43

CHAPTER EIGHT
JESUS CHRIST – THE CENTRALITY OF OUR FAITH   51

CHAPTER NINE
EVER INCREASING FAITH   63

CHAPTER TEN
FAITH/BELIEVE   69

CHAPTER ELEVEN
FAITH AND PERSECUTION   87

CHAPTER TWELVE
THE VICTORIES OF FAITH   93

CHAPTER THIRTEEN
THE VICTORIES OF FAITH II   101

CHAPTER FOURTEEN
THE VICTORIES OF FAITH III   111

OTHER EXCITING TITLES
BY MICHAEL SCANTLEBURY   127

Foreword

Given the sheer volume of good books available on Faith, your initial proclivity might be to devalue the content of the book you have in your hands, on the basis that there's nothing new to learn about the principle of Faith. Well, let me debunk that thought because God's Kingdom's principles are inexhaustible pedagogical goldmines.

I humbly submit that *"Understanding both sides of Faith"* is a masterpiece that will shatter every ceiling the religious culture has set on your Faith and revolutionize your Christian living experience.

When presented with the honor of reading this book by my friend and covenant fellow Apostle Michael Scantlebury, whom I had the privilege of sharing a ministry platform in Australia in 2011, I found myself like a kid in a candy store. The book has been both a tremendous pleasure and a personal blessing.

As a former College educator, a teacher of the subject of Faith and someone who has experienced the benefits of walking by Faith, I can testify to the need for such a book. Michael is an astute anointed penman, with over twenty-five books.

From the onset, he presents the tenets of his tome, by eloquently contrasting the two dimensions of Faith: (1) where we use our Faith to acquire and believe God for new things and victories in Him and (2) where we use that same Faith to resist and battle against all odds that is thrown at us.

After defining the elements of faith, Apostle Michael empowers us with the tools to increase our faith: Our knowledge of God and the application of what we know. It's not enough to know what the Word of God says. What produces real faith is displayed when our actions match our belief.

Through his writing, he reveals to the reader that the power encapsulated within faith is anchored in Jesus-Christ who is the centrality of our faith. Nothing changes until you change it by faith in Jesus. Michael explains to us why faith is a potent force to recon with, as it enables us to walk from glory to glory in our Christian living experience.

Apostle Scantlebury gives us an accurate understanding of the benefits of our trials. Contrary to our Westernized belief, Faith and trials are mutually inclusive. We are encouraged to keep trusting God despite the opposition. Trusting God then becomes the substratum of having a pleasant relationship with Him.

I encourage you to add this book to your personal library as an available resource to prepare and equip you to walk in your victories of Faith. My brother has set before us a full plate. Read, digest, but more importantly, put the principles in this book into practice and become stronger in your faith life, as faith without works is dead.

Apostle Bruner Michael Remy, MBA, MDiv
The Glory Center FL, Inc.
www.tgcflorida.org

Introduction

As we enter this very important subject of Faith, I just wanted to give some credit to my good friend Apostle David Young Snr, who first suggested that I write a book on Faith, as he had read several of my other writings and felt that I had a God-given grace to write. When he said that a 'light' went on inside of me and I knew that I had to, so here is what I came up with. All as a result of my 40+ years of preaching/teaching on the subject of Faith.

Also, please allow me to begin by quoting from the book of Hebrews: Hebrews 11:1-12, 30-40

> *Now faith is the substance of things hoped for, the evidence of things not seen. For by it the elders obtained a good testimony. By faith we understand that the worlds were framed by the word of God, so that the things which are seen were not made of things which are visible. By faith Abel offered to God a more excellent sacrifice than Cain, through which he obtained witness that he was righteous, God testifying of his gifts; and through it he being dead still speaks. By faith Enoch was taken away so that he did not see death, "and was not found, because God had taken him"; for before he was taken he had this testimony, that he pleased God. But without faith it is impossible to please Him, for he who comes to God must believe that He is, and that He is a rewarder of those who diligently seek Him. By faith Noah, being divinely warned of things not yet*

seen, moved with godly fear, prepared an ark for the saving of his household, by which he condemned the world and became heir of the righteousness which is according to faith. By faith Abraham obeyed when he was called to go out to the place which he would receive as an inheritance. And he went out, not knowing where he was going. By faith he dwelt in the land of promise as in a foreign country, dwelling in tents with Isaac and Jacob, the heirs with him of the same promise; for he waited for the city which has foundations, whose builder and maker is God. By faith Sarah herself also received strength to conceive seed, and she bore a child when she was past the age, because she judged Him faithful who had promised. Therefore from one man, and him as good as dead, were born as many as the stars of the sky in multitude—innumerable as the sand which is by the seashore. ... By faith the walls of Jericho fell down after they were encircled for seven days. By faith the harlot Rahab did not perish with those who did not believe, when she had received the spies with peace. And what more shall I say? For the time would fail me to tell of Gideon and Barak and Samson and Jephthah, also of David and Samuel and the prophets: who through faith subdued kingdoms, worked righteousness, obtained promises, stopped the mouths of lions, quenched the violence of fire, escaped the edge of the sword, out of weakness were made strong, became valiant in battle, turned to flight the armies of the aliens. Women received their dead raised to life again. Others were tortured, not accepting deliverance, that they might obtain a better resurrection. Still others had trial of mockings and scourgings, yes, and of chains and imprisonment. They were stoned, they were sawn in two, were tempted, were slain with the sword. They wandered about in sheepskins and goatskins, being destitute, afflicted, tormented—of whom the world was not worthy. They wandered in deserts and mountains, in dens and caves of the earth. And all these, having obtained a good testimony through faith, did not receive the promise, God having provided something better for us, that they should not be made perfect apart from us.*

From this passage we understand that Faith has two dimensions to it:

1. Where we use our *Faith* to acquire and believe God for new things and victories in Him.
2. Where we use that same *Faith* to resist and battle against all odds to resist that which is thrown at us. Thereby becoming stronger in faith as we overcome. We need to know the difference.

So, it is from this premise we approach this tome. Be blessed, inspired, and encouraged as you read/study through these thoughts, which I have presented here!

CHAPTER ONE
FAITH – WHAT IS IT?

WHAT IS FAITH? HEBREWS 11:1 AMP

> *Now Faith is the assurance (the confirmation, the title deed) of the things [we] hope for, being the proof of things [we] do not see and the conviction of their reality [faith perceiving as real fact what is not revealed to the senses].* [Emphasis and Paraphrase Author's]

We can't go anywhere until we deal with the first question: what is faith? Here are a few thoughts that I have heard over the years that I agree with:

1. Faith is confident assurance that God will do what He said He would do.
2. Faith is Biblical evidence of what we cannot see.
3. Faith is the ability to perceive as real what we cannot verify with our senses.

Hebrews 6:11-15 states:

And we desire that each one of you show the same diligence to the full assurance of hope until the end, that you do not become sluggish, but imitate those who through faith and patience inherit the promises. For when God made a promise to Abraham, because He could swear by no one greater, He swore by Himself, saying, "Surely blessing I will bless you, and multiplying I will multiply you." And so, after he had patiently endured, he obtained the promise.

There is a fundamental difference between hope and faith. Hope is 'open-ended,' meaning that it is not tied to anything. You can hope to be successful in life, hope to be healed of a sickness, hope to be promoted, etc. Faith, on the other hand adds substance to this hope. Faith must be tied to God's Word. When we can tie God's Word to what we hope for, then we have confidence that He will do what He said He would do. The Bible tells us that God does not change His mind (Numbers 23:19) and that He cannot lie (Titus 1:2). So, when we substantiate our hope with the Word of God, we can have confidence that He will bring it to pass.

What is Patience? Hebrews 10:36 KJV

For ye have need of patience, that, after ye have done the will of God, ye might receive the promise. [Emphasis Author's]

Most people think of patience as simply waiting. In one sense this is true, but Biblical patience is more specific than simply waiting.

Patience is "**the ability to remain, steadfastly the same, no matter what circumstances may bring our way**." Patience is more than simply waiting on something to happen, but rather remaining the same while you wait. You can see how this ability, coupled with faith, is very important.

Because as we steadfastly wait on the fulfilment of the promise from God, the enemy will make every attempt to get you to lose heart during that 'waiting time'. He will tell you that God is not going to do it, that He did not hear your prayer, that you need to lower your expectations, etc., etc...

This ability to remain the same (patience) will enable you to combat the thoughts of fear, doubt, and unbelief; and make it possible for you to remain in faith.

James 1:4 AMP says:

But let endurance and steadfastness and patience have full play and do a thorough work, so that you may be perfectly and fully *developed [**with no defects**], lacking in nothing.* [Emphasis and Paraphrase Author's]

What is the big deal about patience? Well, **the issue is not whether you know how to suffer, or whether you know how to endure pain; the issue is whether or not you can be trusted to remain faithful for the long run.** Does God know that you have the ability to remain the same, no matter what the devil may attack you with? That is the key issue.

If we search the Scriptures to find people that God used mightily you will see a common denominator in all of their lives – they were people that were **proven faithful**. Here are just a few examples:

- Abraham proved himself faithful when he was willing to offer God his only son.
- Noah proved himself faithful when he continued to seek God, even though he was surrounded by a world of heathens.
- David proved himself faithful while he was a shepherd boy and protected his sheep from a lion and a bear.
- Elisha proved himself faithful to serve Elijah for many years before he received his anointing. And the list could go on.

Remember this:

- Happiness is a result of happenings; joy is a fruit of the Spirit (Galatians 5:22).
- Happiness is only available when something good happens, and then only for a temporary period. Once happiness is over, it is over.
- However, joy is a by-product of the presence of the Holy Spirit and is always available to those who are Born-Again.

When unbelievers face difficulties they have to endure them without having the ability to tap into happiness. On the other hand, Believers can face difficulties with the Holy Spirit and can therefore tap into Joy. A Believer can always rejoice (Philippians 4:4), but an unbeliever can never be in a state of happiness all the time, specially in difficult/trying circumstances.

What good is your faith if has not been tested? **Tested faith is proven faith**: When challenges come your way don't look at them as an overwhelming obstacle, but rather face them in faith. Every test is an opportunity to exercise your faith and to prove your faith in that area.

NOW REMEMBER THIS: FAITH WORKS WITH PATIENCE!
Patience: The ability to remain steadfast, to continue pressing on and pressing in with a calm assurance and a bold confidence, regardless of the adversity or the length of time that has transpired, knowing that what God has said will surely come to pass.

It is the Greek word "makrothumia" and is rendered – to be long-winded or long-spirited; having fortitude; longsuffering; with long enduring temper. Steadfastness, consistency, endurance; the characteristic of someone who is not swerved from their deliberate purpose and loyalty to faith, even the greatest trials and sufferings; a patient enduring, sustaining, perseverance.

1. **Faith and patience are the actual instruments through which the promises of God are received for our lives!**
    a. They work together – It takes a man and a woman to produce a child. For the sperm and the egg to produce new life; they must go together.
    b. Hebrews 11:1 "Faith is now" – faith sees the end from the beginning.

    - Because "*faith is now*", if from the moment a woman conceives the child, and until it's birth it would be a matter of seconds instead of months that would be disastrous!
    - Think of the contortions that woman's body would go through stretching and chemical changes. It would devastate her physically, mentally and emotionally. It would be impossible for her to adjust to all the phenomenal changes so suddenly.
    - In spiritual terms, that is exactly what would happen if the dream or vision God put in our heart manifested instantly. We would be unprepared to carry it forth.
    - James 1:3-4 "Knowing that the testing of your faith produces patience. But let patience have *its* perfect work, that you may be perfect and complete, lacking nothing."

2. Patience brings God's perfect timing into the picture.
   a. Without patience there is no "Due Season!"
   b. "Due Season" means exactly the right time, both for us, and the full manifestation of our dream. Galatians 6:9

And let us not grow weary while doing good, for in due season we shall reap if we do not lose heart.

3. God knows.
   a. We need time to adjust to all the changes in our lives that are products of fulfilling our vision.
   b. We must build up our muscle of faith: it's the sustaining force of our life.
   c. It brings forth perfection and maturity into our lives.

4. Fulfilling our dreams and God's purpose for our lives will require us to adjust.
   a. Wrong attitudes must be discarded – God will work on our actions and reactions.
   b. We will be required to stretch in ways we never thought possible.
   c. Our motives will be challenged.

5. What can we do now? Patience is not passive.
   a. Begin now to prepare for what God has told us to do.
   b. It will take the blessing and anointing of God and a lot of hard work.
   c. At the very core of God's being is faithfulness – what God has promised – He will perform – He will do what He promised.

As we continue believing the Lord for the move of His Spirit in this territory let us hold fast our profession of Faith patiently to the very fulfilling of every purpose the Lord has purposed for us.

NOW FAITH IS!
Hebrews 11:1

<u>Now faith is</u> *the substance of things hoped for, the evidence of things not seen.* [Emphasis Author's]

The very foundation of faith is trust.

Allow Me A Moment to Share This Story with You:

Blanch Taylor Moore (born in 1933 and is currently still on death row in North Carolina) was a woman who was loved and trusted by many men. When her third husband became very ill and was hospitalized, the doctors couldn't find what was causing him to be so ill. Finally, a doctor ran some tests that revealed a very high arsenic level. The police were informed and they suspected his wife. He wouldn't hear of it. She had nursed him and cared for him during his illness and he trusted her. The more the police dug into her past the more they suspected her. Finally, after exhuming the bodies of her first two husbands and her father and finding out that they all died of arsenic poisoning, they arrested her. She was tried and convicted of murder.

The story of Blanch Taylor Moore is a classical story of trust betrayed. A wife, who one loves and trusts, proves to be a murderer. A wife, who one trusts as their best friend, proves to be no friend at all, but an enemy. This happens over and over in human experiences. A story like this reminds us of a very basic and simple fact of life, and that fact is this; **all of our valuable relationships in life are built on trust**.

- When a husband and wife stop trusting each other, they may continue to be married, but they can no longer have a happy marriage.
- When two friends stop trusting each other, they may continue to see each other, but they no longer have a true friendship.

Now, if that is true in our human relationships, how much truer is it in our relationship to God?

In one of the truly great statements of the Bible, the writer of Hebrews tells us, **_Without faith it is impossible to please God_** (Hebrews 11:6). There is no way our relationship to God can be pleasing to Him unless we trust Him.

Do I need to remind you that this is where it all begins for us? The way that we became a Christian in the first place was by an act of faith, an act of trust.

Think about it for a moment: When I come to the living God as a guilty sinner, deserving hell, but trusting in Jesus Christ and Him alone for my redemption, at that point I am engaged in an act of faith.

- Remember, I've never seen God.
- I've never seen this place called "Heaven", or this place called "hell".
- I've never seen Jesus Christ.

However, by faith, those things which I cannot see become realities to me. They take on substance for me, and by faith, I gain assurance and conviction about things that my eyes cannot behold. That is what faith is all about.

But trusting God for my eternal salvation is only the beginning. It is the start of a journey that cannot be travelled successfully in any other way but by a **growing faith**.

Hence, we must distinguish between saving faith and the faith of obedience, which causes us to grow in God. Thousands of Believers have trusted Christ for their salvation but are not living in faith trusting God in each and every area of their lives.

As we come to chapter 11 in the book of Hebrews, it is very evident that the subject is faith. But it is very important that we be aware of the connection between chapter 10 and 11 as we study the nature of faith in chapter 11. We must study it in context.

As we examine the context, we see that the writer of the book of Hebrews is not talking about saving faith but he is taking about living faith, not faith in God for our eternal life but faith in God to carry us through our daily lives.

Again, please remember, the author of Hebrews is writing to Hebrew Christians who are suffering great persecution from the hand of their Jewish brothers. They were discouraged and on the verge of turning away from Christianity and going back to Judaism. He is exhorting them to endurance in their Christian lives:

Hebrews 10:35-36

> *Therefore do not cast away your confidence, which has great reward. For you have need of endurance, so that after you have done the will of God, you may receive the promise:*

In the midst of trials and persecution a person's faith may waver, or they may even turn from their faith. Luke talks about this in:

Luke 8:13

But the ones on the rock are those who, when they hear, receive the word with joy; and these have no root, who believe for a while and in time of temptation fall away.

Hence, the reason for the exhortation to endure in faith:
Hebrews 3:18-19

And to whom did He swear that they would not enter His rest, but to those who did not obey? So we see that they could not enter in because of unbelief.

Hebrews 4:1-2

Therefore, since <u>a promise remains of entering His rest</u>, let us fear lest any of you seem to have come short of it. For indeed the <u>gospel</u> was preached to us as well as to them; but the word which they heard did not profit them, not being mixed with faith in those who heard it. [Emphasis Author's]

The word "**gospel**" is the Greek word *euaggelizo*, a verb, which means: "**to announce good news**."

The character of the Good News must be defined by the context. "Gospel" doesn't always mean the plan of salvation. In Hebrews 4:2, it is used of Good News of the Promised Rest as in:

Hebrews 4:6

Since therefore it remains that some must enter it, and those to whom it was first preached [<u>euaggelizo</u>] *did not enter because of disobedience,* [Emphasis and Parenthesis Author's]

In Hebrews 4:2 it says, *"...**the gospel was preached to us as well as to them....**"* – "<u>us</u>" here is referring to the writer of Hebrews and its readers, and the "<u>them</u>" refers to Israelites back in the wilderness. The "<u>**Good News**</u>" they heard about was of no value to them, because of their lack of faith:

Hebrews 3:19

So we see that they could not enter in because of unbelief.

If we understand this letter as a call to go on believing in the truths of Christianity, this chapter (11) makes a lot of sense. **It's not an explanation of how to be saved**. It is rather a call to perseverance in faith, whatever the odds, whatever the situation that one is faced with!
Hebrews 10:38

Now the <u>just</u> shall live by faith; But if anyone draws back, My soul has no pleasure in him. [Emphasis Author's]

The word "<u>**just**</u>" is from the Greek ***dikaios***, which means: "**righteous or the sanctified**." It is referring to Believers. Believers are to live by faith – dependent trust upon God. That sentence in Hebrews 10:38 really forms the text of which Hebrews 11 is the sermon.

The central design of this chapter is to demonstrate the endurance of those who, in the past, endured by faith before they received the fulfillment of God's promises:
Hebrews 11:35

Women received their dead raised to life again. And others were tortured, not accepting deliverance, that they might obtain a better resurrection.

The author concludes chapter 10 by saying, *"But if anyone draws back,* (from living by faith) *My soul has no pleasure in him."* This is because faith pleases God (Hebrews 11:6).
Hebrews 10:39

But we are not of those who draw back to perdition, but of those who believe to the saving of the (life) soul.

The phrase "**saving the soul**" is probably best translated: "**preserving of the life**."

Chapter 11 is an extended list of examples of Old Testament men and women who lived by faith and preserved their lives. As we all know the

Scriptures were not originally written with chapter and verse, these were added in later; so, I would say: This is really not a good place for a chapter break.

Hebrews 11:1

Now faith is the substance of things hoped for, the evidence of things not seen. [Emphasis Author's]

"Now faith is" – this verse is not a definition of faith; it is a description. Before we go deeper into this chapter, we must understand what faith is.

I would dare say that most Believers couldn't explain what faith is if they were asked. **Do you know what faith is?** If someone asked you what faith is, could you explain it to them? Before we look at what faith is, let's dispel some myths.

WHAT FAITH IS NOT:
- Some say that we live by faith every day.
- You turn on your faucet, fill a glass of water and drink it – that's faith.
- You open a can of food and you eat it – that's faith.
- Or you fly in an airplane – that's faith.

Hear me – those things are not faith! That is simply putting into practice what is called the law of mathematical probability.

You are saying to yourself, "Well, thousands of people do this every day and everything is all right, so I'll do the same."

I've grown up seeing people drink out of the faucet – that is not faith.

Faith is not **superstition**; it's not a sort of sixth sense, some intuition into the spiritual realm, or an open sesame sort of thing.

Faith is not **wishful thinking** – I want a certain thing to happen, so I'm having faith that it will.

Many people are like the girl who was asked to define faith. She said, "Faith is believing what you know isn't so." That is what faith is to many. They think it is some sort of gamble. That is not faith. Faith is always **intelligent**; it knows what it is doing.

BIBLICALLY DEFINED, FAITH IS UNDERSTANDING AND AN AGREEMENT TO A PROPOSITION.

For example: If you were to ask me, "Where is my money?" And I said to you, "The check is in the mail." Now, you are either going to believe me, which is faith; you are trusting in what I said, or you are not. No matter what the subject, whether it be God or guns, the psychology or linguistics of belief is identical in all cases.

Faith must begin with knowledge; you cannot believe what you don't know or understand. Belief is the act of assenting to something understood. But understanding alone is not belief in what is understood. For example: I understand the teaching of evolution, but I do not assent to it. I understand Dispensational theology, but I do not believe it.

Now hear this: Soren Kierkegard, a Dutch theologian of the mid nineteenth century, has greatly influenced the Church's thinking. He taught that it really makes no difference "what" we believe. The "what" is unimportant, all that counts is the "how." There are not different ways of believing; there are only different things to believe in. We often hear people say, "They are so sincere in their faith." But if they believe the wrong thing, they are sincerely wrong!

The Church has taken Kierkegard's teaching of "how" and come up with "head" and "heart" belief. They ask, "Do you believe it with your head or heart?" However, the Bible makes no such distinction. Scripture never contrasts the head and the heart, but frequently contrasts the heart and the lips. For example, here is what it says in Romans 10:8-10

> But what does it say? "<u>The word is near you, in your mouth and in your heart</u>" (that is, the word of faith which we preach): that if you confess with your mouth the Lord Jesus and believe in your heart that God has raised Him from the dead, you will be saved. For with the heart one believes unto righteousness, and with the mouth confession is made unto salvation. [Emphasis Author's]

FAITH IS BELIEVING A PROMISE:
Romans 4:20-21

> He did not waver at the <u>promise of God</u> through unbelief, but was strengthened in faith, giving glory to God, and being fully convinced

that what He had promised *He was also able to perform.* [Emphasis Author's]

Abraham understood what God was promising him, and he believed Him. **Faith must have a promise**. Believing God for things He hasn't promised isn't faith, it's presumption or foolishness.
John 11:23-27

Jesus said to her, "Your brother will rise again." Martha said to Him, "I know that he will rise again in the resurrection at the last day." Jesus said to her, "I am the resurrection and the life. He who believes in Me, though he may die, he shall live. "And whoever lives and believes in Me shall never die. Do you believe this?" She said to Him, "Yes, Lord, I believe that You are the Christ, the Son of God, who is to come into the world."

She understood what Jesus was saying, and she believed Him – this is faith. And it is faith that brings eternal life:
John 20:31

but these are written that you may believe that Jesus is the Christ, the Son of God, and that believing you may have life in His name.

In our next chapter we would explore some things about Faith. So, here we go…

Let's check our understanding of the Chapter "Faith – What is it?"

1. What does the word "Faith" mean to you? Is it different from the biblical definition of the word in Hebrew 11:1?

2. How is Hope different from Faith?

3. In what circumstances can we be assured that God will bring to pass a particular hope we hold on to?

4. How is the biblical definition of "patience" different from that of our usual understanding of this word?

5. Why do you believe God wants us to be patient in-order to receive the things He has promised us?

6. What is the Greek word translated "patience" in Scripture?

7. What are the 2 essential characteristics that we need to possess in-order to receive Gods promises for our lives? Explain.

8. Based on the definition of Faith in Heb.11:1, what is the foundation of faith?

9. Do you believe the statement "Without faith it is impossible to please God" (Hebrews 11:6) to be one of the most profound statements in the Bible? Why?

10. What is the difference between saving faith and the faith of obedience/living faith?

11. What is the Greek word for "gospel"? What does it mean based on the different context it is being used in Hebrews 4:2 and 4:6?

12. What does the Greek word "dikaios" mean?

13. To whom does the writer of Hebrews refer to as just?

14. How is faith different from "Superstition", "wishful thinking" or believing in something that you are totally unaware of?

15. What is your response to "you cannot believe what you don't know or understand. Belief is the act of assenting to something understood. But understanding alone is not belief in what is understood".?

16. Explain "Faith must have a Promise"

Chapter Two
Some Things About Faith

Let me share with you three things about faith that we must understand:

1. SAVING FAITH IS SUPERNATURAL.
John 12:36-40

> *"While you have the light, believe in the light, that you may become sons of light." These things Jesus spoke, and departed, and was hidden from them. But although He had done so many signs before them, they did not believe in Him, that the word of Isaiah the prophet might be fulfilled, which he spoke: "Lord, who has believed our report? And to whom has the arm of the LORD been revealed?"* <u>Therefore, they could not believe</u>, *because Isaiah said again: "He has blinded their eyes and hardened their hearts, lest they should see with their eyes, lest they should understand with their hearts and turn, So that I should heal them."* [Emphasis Author's]

Unregenerate man is unable to believe the gospel. He is blinded by sin. 1 Corinthians 2:14

> *But the natural man does not receive the things of the Spirit of God, for they are foolishness to him; nor can he know them, because they are spiritually discerned.*

Man is spiritually dead and cannot believe until God gives him spiritual life.

Ephesians 2:1

And you He made alive, who were dead in trespasses and sins, [Emphasis Author's]

Ephesians 2:8

For by grace, you have been saved through faith, and that not of yourselves; it is the gift of God, [Emphasis Author's]

Faith is a gift of God. Saving faith is supernatural. Man cannot believe apart from God's work of regeneration.

2. ASSURANCE IS AN IMPORTANT PART OF SAVING FAITH.

Faith always has in it the element of assurance (a confident knowing). Do you have the assurance that you will spend eternity in Heaven? The answer should be a resounding YES!

John 5:24

Most assuredly, I say to you, he who hears My word and believes in Him who sent Me has everlasting life, and shall not come into judgment, but has passed from death into life.

John 6:47

Most assuredly, I say to you, he who believes in Me has everlasting life.

If I believe in Jesus Christ, what does He promise me? Everlasting life! So, if I doubt my eternal destiny, I am not believing Jesus Christ.

Assurance is necessarily a part of believing the gospel. Jesus Christ offers a guarantee to everyone who believes in Him. If I base my assurance on how I live, I'm trusting me and not Jesus Christ.

3. THERE ARE DEGREES OF FAITH:

We often think in terms of you either have faith or you don't. But the Bible talks of various degrees of faith.

Romans 4:19-20

And not being weak in faith, he did not consider his own body, already dead (since he was about a hundred years old), and the deadness of Sarah's womb. <u>He did not waver at the promise of God</u> *through unbelief, but was strengthened in faith, giving glory to God,* [Emphasis Author's]

The New American Standard Bible puts it this way:
Romans 4:20 (NASB)

<u>yet, with respect to the promise of God, he did not waver</u> *in unbelief, but grew strong in faith, giving glory to God,* [Emphasis Author's]

So, we understand that Abraham did not have "**weak**" faith, his faith was "**strong**." This shows that there are degrees of faith. Our Lord charges the disciples in general, and Peter in particular, as having "little faith." They had faith, but unlike Abraham's, it was deficient in strength:

Matthew 6:30

Now if God so clothes the grass of the field, which today is, and tomorrow is thrown into the oven, will He not much more clothe you, O you of <u>little faith</u>*?* [Emphasis Author's]

Matthew 14:31 Speaking about Peter, walking on the water...

And immediately Jesus stretched out His hand and caught him, and said to him, "O you of <u>little faith</u>*, why did you doubt?"* [Emphasis Author's]

As Peter focused on the circumstances around him (the wind and the waves) instead of on Christ, his faith grew weak. I'll bet that most of you can relate to this; can't you? When you are focusing on the circumstances, doesn't your faith grow weak?

Jesus said that the centurion had "**great**" faith:
Matthew 8:10

"When Jesus heard it, He marveled, and said to those who followed, "Assuredly, I say to you, I have not found such **great faith***, not even in Israel!"*

The Apostles asked Jesus to increase their faith:
Luke 17:5

And the apostles said to the Lord, "Increase our faith." [Emphasis Author's]

In Acts 6:8, Stephen was said to be *"**full of faith**."* The Greek word for "full" is *pleres*, which means: "complete or mature".

In 1 Thessalonians 3:10, Paul said he wanted to perfect that which was lacking in their faith. "night and day praying exceedingly that we may see your face and **perfect what is lacking in your faith**?"

In 2 Thessalonians 1:3, Paul said, *"Your faith grows exceedingly."*

We are bound to thank God always for you, brethren, as it is fitting, because your faith grows exceedingly, *and the love of every one of you all abounds toward each other,* [Emphasis Author's]

James talks about "dead" faith in James 2:17, 20

Thus also faith by itself, if it does not have works, is dead. ... But do you want to know, O foolish man, that faith without works is dead?

And he talks about "mature" faith in James 2:22

Do you see that faith was working together with his works, and by works faith was made perfect (or mature)? [Emphasis and Parenthesis Author's]

So, we can see that the Scriptures speak of several types and levels of Faith:

- **Little Faith – Matthew 8:26**
- **Great Faith – Matthew 8:10**
- **Weak Faith – Romans 14:1**
- **Strong Faith – Romans 4:19-20**
- **Lacking Faith – Mark 4:40**
- **Perfect Faith – 2 Timothy 1:5, James 2:22**
- **Dead Faith – James 2:14-17**
- **Rich Faith – James 2:5**
- **Full Faith – Acts 11:24**
- **Growing Faith, and – Romans 1:17**
- **Increasing Faith – Luke 17:5**

There are degrees of faith. All Believers don't have the same amount of faith. Some Believers are weak in faith. Some Believers have dead faith.

Let me show you another example of strong faith:
John 4:46-47

So Jesus came again to Cana of Galilee where He had made the water wine. And there was a certain nobleman whose son was sick at Capernaum. When he heard that Jesus had come out of Judea into Galilee, he went to Him and implored Him to come down and heal his son, for he was at the point of death.

If you had a child that was dying, what would you do? Would you trust Christ no matter what happened?
John 4:48

Then Jesus said to him, "Unless you people see signs and wonders, you will by no means believe."

Jesus was concerned that the man's faith was based only on signs and wonders.
John 4:49

The nobleman said to Him, "Sir, come down before my child dies!"

The nobleman compelled Christ to act, but Christ simply spoke the word:

John 4:50

Jesus said to him, "<u>Go your way; your son lives</u>." So the <u>man believed the word</u> that Jesus spoke to him, and he went his way." [Emphasis Author's]

The man believed what Christ said, *"Your son lives."* He understood what Christ was saying and he believed it. What would you do at this point? Would you run all the way home? Won't that be a sign of weak faith – looking for proof.

John 4:51-52

And as he was now going down, his servants met him and told him, saying, "<u>Your son lives!</u>" Then he inquired of them the hour when he got better. And they said to him, "<u>Yesterday at the seventh hour the fever left him</u>." [Emphasis Author's]

The man asks when his son got better and he was told, *"Yesterday."*

Now hear this: If you were to look at a map, Cana and Capernaum were only a short distance apart (about 16 miles), the journey could have easily been made in about four hours in those days. It was between 1-2pm (Roman time) when Jesus pronounced the boy healed. Such strong faith had the nobleman in Christ's word that he didn't return home until the next day. That is strong faith!

The more you walk in faith, the more you walk in victory and joy, so we need to learn to live by faith. Faith pleases God.

In our next chapter we would look at how we can increase our Faith.

Let's check our Understanding of the Chapter "Some Things About Faith."

1. The author talks about 3 important characteristics of Faith. What are they?

2. Explain in brief your understanding of John 12:36-40?

3. What causes the unregenerate man to be blinded? Explain with scriptural reference/s

4. Why is assurance important in saving faith?

5. What is the guarantee that Jesus Christ offers to those who believe in Him?

6. Which passages in the Bible talks of different types/degrees of faith?

7. What is the Greek word translated "full" in Acts 6:8? What is its meaning?

8. Reflect – Are you walking through life in Strong Faith? Or Are you of Little Faith being swayed by every wind unable to enjoy victory and joy in life?

CHAPTER THREE
HOW CAN WE INCREASE OUR FAITH?

THERE ARE TWO MAIN FACTORS, WHICH DETERMINE THE STRENGTH OF OUR FAITH.

FIRST, IS OUR KNOWLEDGE OF GOD:
The main explanation of the troubles and difficulties, which most Christians experience in their lives, is due to a lack of knowledge about God. We need to study the revelation that God has given of Himself and of His Character. That is how to develop strong faith. The more you know God, the more you will trust Him.

Martin Luther said to Erasmus, "Your thoughts of God are too human." I think that is true of most Christians.

Romans 10:17

So then faith comes by hearing, and hearing by the word of God.
[Emphasis Author's]

We need to study the Word that we may know Him. It's hard to trust someone you don't know.

THE SECOND ELEMENT IS THE APPLICATION OF WHAT WE KNOW:
A knowledge that never ventures out upon what it knows will never be a strong faith.

Luke 8:22-25

Now it happened, on a certain day, that He got into a boat with His disciples. And He said to them, "Let us cross over to the other side of the lake." And they launched out. But as they sailed He fell asleep. And a windstorm came down on the lake, and they were filling with water, and were in jeopardy. And they came to Him and awoke Him, saying, "Master, Master, we are perishing!" Then He arose and rebuked the wind and the raging of the water. And they ceased, and there was a calm. But He said to them, "<u>Where is your faith?</u>" And they were afraid, and marveled, saying to one another, "Who can this be? For He commands even the winds and water, and they obey Him!"

The Disciples who were in the boat during the storm were failing to apply their faith and that is why our Lord put His question to them in that particular form. He said, "**<u>Where is your faith?</u>**"

- They had faith, but where was it?
- Why weren't they applying it to the situation that they were in?

Their problem was, they did not use the faith they had. I suppose they didn't think that it was applicable in that situation… I guess that for some reason they did not think it would work, that God would not respond to them…

They were looking at the waves and the water coming in the boat. They were bailing it out, but still more was coming in and they cried out to Jesus, "We're going to die." He said to them, "**<u>Where is your faith?</u>**" And He was right, After all they had seen Jesus do the miraculous, they should have trusted Him:

Luke 7:12-15

And when He came near the gate of the city, behold, a dead man was being carried out, the only son of his mother; and she was a widow. And a large crowd from the city was with her. When the Lord saw her, He had compassion on her and said to her, "Do not weep." Then He came and touched the open coffin, and those who carried him stood still. And He said, "Young man, I say to you, arise." So he who was dead sat up and began to speak. And He presented him to his mother.

They saw Jesus raise the dead, and they were worried about drowning? They weren't applying their faith. In addition to our knowledge of God, there is this very important element – **we must apply what we know.**

At times we do apply what we know, and we come through the problems and difficulties victorious. We operate like David when he faced Goliath. Yet at other times we become so consumed with our circumstances, and in those moments, we do not apply our faith; like David before Achish the king of Gath.

David was scared to death, and he changed his behavior and pretended he was crazy. He began to scribble on the doors and drool all over himself **– 1 Samuel 21:10-14**

> *Then David arose and fled that day from before Saul, and went to Achish the king of Gath. And the servants of Achish said to him, "Is this not David the king of the land? Did they not sing of him to one another in dances, saying: 'Saul has slain his thousands, And David his ten thousands'?" Now David took these words to heart, and was very much afraid of Achish the king of Gath. ¹³ So he changed his behavior before them, pretended madness in their hands, scratched on the doors of the gate, and let his saliva fall down on his beard. Then Achish said to his servants, "Look, you see the man is insane.*

What happened to the giant killer? He wasn't applying his faith. He forgot about his God. Have you ever done that? You think your faith is strong; then you have a trial, a situation that causes you to panic and drool all over yourself. At those times we need to focus on God to meditate on Him and apply what we know:

Hebrews 13:5

> *Let your conduct be without covetousness; be content with such things as you have. For He Himself has said, "<u>I will never leave you nor forsake you.</u>"* [Emphasis Author's]

That is a promise from the Sovereign God of the Universe. He is always with us.

When we fail to trust God, we doubt His Sovereignty and question His Goodness. God views our distrust as seriously as He views our disobedience. When the Children of Israel were hungry, they spoke against God:

Psalms 78:19-21

Yes, they spoke against God: They said, "Can God prepare a table in the wilderness? Behold, He struck the rock, So that the waters gushed out, And the streams overflowed. Can He give bread also? Can He provide meat for His people?" Therefore, the LORD heard this and was furious; So a fire was kindled against Jacob, And anger also came up against Israel,

Why was it that God was so angry with them?
Psalms 78:22

Because they did not believe in God, And did not trust in His salvation.

In order to trust God, we must always view our adverse circumstances through the eyes of faith. Faith pleases God.

Many folks have reduced Christianity to a bunch of rules; do this and don't do that. They think they are pleasing God simply by doing things and not doing other things. However, I would like for you to listen to this: the thing that most pleases God is our faith in Him. We are to live by faith, trusting Him in every situation of life.

Let's check our Understanding of the Chapter 3 - "How Can We Increase Our Faith."

1. What 2 main factors determines the strength of our faith?

2. Do you believe it is important to apply what we know in our daily lives? Why?

3. Which Scripture promises us that God will never leave us nor forsake us?

4. How is it possible for us/what should we do to have the capacity to trust God in adverse circumstances?

CHAPTER FOUR
Faith to Obtain

We would begin this chapter with the following passages:

Romans 12:3

For I say, through the grace given to me, to everyone who is among you, not to think of himself more highly than he ought to think, but to think soberly, as God has dealt to each one a measure of faith.

Romans 1:17

For in it the righteousness of God is revealed from faith to faith; as it is written, "The just shall live by faith."

Romans 14:23

But he who doubts is condemned if he eats, because he does not eat from faith; for whatever is not from faith is sin.

Everyone starts out with the same measure of FAITH: I believe according to Romans 12:3.

I have the same measure as the great heroes of the faith.

Faith increases or decreases based on what we do with it. BUT EVERYONE STARTS OUT WITH THE SAME MEASURE OF FAITH.

Matthew 17:14-20 especially verse 20 states the following:

And when they had come to the multitude, a man came to Him, kneeling down to Him and saying, "Lord, have mercy on my son, for he is an epileptic and suffers severely; for he often falls into the fire and often into the water. So I brought him to Your disciples, but they could not cure him." Then Jesus answered and said, "O faithless and perverse generation, how long shall I be with you? How long shall I bear with you? Bring him here to Me." And Jesus rebuked the demon, and it came out of him; and the child was cured from that very hour. Then the disciples came to Jesus privately and said, "Why could we not cast it out?" So Jesus said to them, "Because of your unbelief; for assuredly, I say to you, if you have faith as a mustard seed, you will say to this mountain, 'Move from here to there,' and it will move; and nothing will be impossible for you." [Emphasis Author's]

It is not whom you know that will get you places, but it is dependent upon the quality of your Faith!

<u>Hebrews 11:6</u>

But without faith it is impossible to please Him, for he who comes to God must believe that He is, and that He is a rewarder of those who diligently seek Him.

Rewarder: It is the Greek word "misthapodosia" (mis-thap-od-ot-ace) and it means to hire for a wage, reward, or salary.

God Does Not Respond To The Following:

1. Crying & Tears: only if it is in conjunction with our faith.
2. Fears: even if they are legitimate ones
3. Hope: The devil and the world like this, because it pushes everything for the future (one day this or that will happen) God is a today; now God! <u>HEBREWS 4:1-7 FAITH RECEIVES; HOPE WAITS!</u>
4. Patience: even though we may think so God DOES NOT RESPOND to our patience. Patience is a by-product of our FAITH. James 1:3 *knowing that the testing of your faith produces patience.*

Let's check our Understanding of the Chapter 4 - "Faith to Obtain."

1. Do you agree with the author that everyone starts with the same measure of faith? Explain with scriptural references.

2. What is the relationship between faith and those who are considered just by God?

3. How does lack of faith affect our individual lives?

4. What is your understanding of Hebrews 11:6?

5. According to the author, what are some of the things that God does not respond to?

CHAPTER FIVE
NOTHING CHANGES UNTIL YOU CHANGE IT BY FAITH IN JESUS

IF YOU DO NOT LIKE YOUR PRESENT CIRCUMSTANCE, CHANGE IT! THERE IS AN onus upon YOU:

- Faith comes by hearing the Word of God,
- Faith increases by doing the word of God,
- We receive when we do the Word of God by Faith.

1 Timothy 4:8

For bodily exercise profits a little, but godliness is profitable for all things, having promise of the life that now is and of that which is to come.

GODLINESS PROFITS ALL THINGS, FOR US:
What a tremendous investment:
Profits ALL; not some, but ALL! (all and only all is all that all will ever be whenever we are speaking about ALL; All means All!)
However, some people cannot handle the blessings if God were to give it to you right now. Let me ask you a couple questions.

1: If God were to prosper you financially right now would you still be willing to turn up in service next Sunday morning?
2: Would you invest in the things of God, by supporting the preaching of the Gospel?
3: What you really do if God were to prosper you financially right now?

Some people say, well I would give so much to the work of God, but when you check them out right now, they are not giving, guess what?
Luke 16:1-13

> He also said to His disciples: "There was a certain rich man who had a steward, and an accusation was brought to him that this man was wasting his goods. So he called him and said to him, 'What is this I hear about you? Give an account of your stewardship, for you can no longer be steward.' "Then the steward said within himself, 'What shall I do? For my master is taking the stewardship away from me. I cannot dig; I am ashamed to beg. I have resolved what to do, that when I am put out of the stewardship, they may receive me into their houses.' "So he called every one of his master's debtors to him, and said to the first, 'How much do you owe my master?' And he said, 'A hundred measures of oil.' So he said to him, 'Take your bill, and sit down quickly and write fifty.' Then he said to another, 'And how much do you owe?' So he said, 'A hundred measures of wheat.' And he said to him, 'Take your bill, and write eighty.' So the master commended the unjust steward because he had dealt shrewdly. For the sons of this world are more shrewd in their generation than the sons of light. "And I say to you, make friends for yourselves by unrighteous mammon, that when you fail, they may receive you into an everlasting home. He who is faithful in what is least, is faithful also in much; and he who is unjust in what is least is unjust also in much. Therefore if you have not been faithful in the unrighteous mammon, who will commit to your trust the true riches? And if you have not been faithful in what is another man's, who will give you what is your own? "No servant can serve two masters; for either he will hate the one and love the other, or else he will be loyal to the one and despise the other. You cannot serve God and mammon."

Hebrews 11:33

who through faith subdued kingdoms, worked righteousness, obtained promises, stopped the mouths of lions,

Some things FAITH likes to DO!

1. Faith likes to conquer: - it conquers, poverty, rebellion, boredom, demonic Spirits, etc.
2. Faith likes to work or bring about Righteousness: - Righteous Living.
3. Faith likes to OBTAIN Promises: - most people like this but they do not like to conquer and work.
4. Faith likes to STOP, whether is a false accusation, or a lying tongue or a demonic voice, it likes to stop.
5. Faith likes to Quench the violence of fire: - that is demonic fire.
6. Escape the edge of the Sword.
7. Out of Weakness to rise up strong.
8. Become Valiant in fight.
9. Put to fight the enemy.
10. Cause that which was dead to live again, whether it is your marriage, your health, your relationship, your desire for the things of God, faith can cause it to live again.

FAITH IS A POTENT FORCE!

It is like the space shuttle that takes a great amount of energy to lift off, in its first stages, ~~then~~ than at any other point of its orbit. In the same manner we need to take a leap of faith if we are going to fully experience God.

STARTING IS TOUGH and it COSTS!

Next, we want to look at these heroes of Faith and glean some principles from their lives.

Let's check our Understanding of the Chapter 5 - "Nothing Changes until You Change it by faith in Jesus."

1. Do you agree with the author on what is required of us in-order to change our circumstances and "receive" from God?

2. According to 1 Timothy 4:8 what does it profit for a person to exercise their spiritual muscle?

3. What is your understanding of Luke 16:1-13?

4. What does the aforementioned parable teach us as to how we should order our footsteps upon this earth?

5. Can you name some of the characteristics of faith?

6. The author states that "Faith is a potent force!". Do you agree? Explain

CHAPTER SIX
HEROES OF FAITH

HEBREWS 11:4-12, 17-30

By faith Abel offered to God a more excellent sacrifice than Cain, through which he obtained witness that he was righteous, God testifying of his gifts; and through it he being dead still speaks. By faith Enoch was taken away so that he did not see death, "and was not found, because God had taken him"; for before he was taken he had this testimony, that he pleased God. But without faith it is impossible to please Him, for he who comes to God must believe that He is, and that He is a rewarder of those who diligently seek Him. By faith Noah, being divinely warned of things not yet seen, moved with godly fear, prepared an ark for the saving of his household, by which he condemned the world and became heir of the righteousness which is according to faith. By faith Abraham obeyed when he was called to go out to the place which he would receive as an inheritance. And he went out, not knowing where he was going. By faith he dwelt in the land of promise as in a foreign country, dwelling in tents with Isaac and Jacob, the heirs with him of the same promise; for he waited for the city which has foundations, whose builder and maker is God. By faith Sarah herself also received strength to conceive seed, and she bore a child when she was past the age, because she judged Him faithful who had promised. Therefore from one man, and him as good as dead, were born as many as the stars of the sky in multitude—innumerable as the sand which is by the seashore.

By faith Abraham, when he was tested, offered up Isaac, and he who had received the promises offered up his only begotten son, of whom it was said, "In Isaac your seed shall be called," concluding that God was able to raise him up, even from the dead, from which he also received him in a figurative sense. By faith Isaac blessed Jacob and Esau concerning things to come. By faith Jacob, when he was dying, blessed each of the sons of Joseph, and worshiped, leaning on the top of his staff. By faith Joseph, when he was dying, made mention of the departure of the children of Israel, and gave instructions concerning his bones. By faith Moses, when he was born, was hidden three months by his parents, because they saw he was a beautiful child; and they were not afraid of the king's command. By faith Moses, when he became of age, refused to be called the son of Pharaoh's daughter, choosing rather to suffer affliction with the people of God than to enjoy the passing pleasures of sin, esteeming the reproach of Christ greater riches than the treasures in Egypt; for he looked to the reward. By faith he forsook Egypt, not fearing the wrath of the king; for he endured as seeing Him who is invisible. By faith he kept the Passover and the sprinkling of blood, lest he who destroyed the firstborn should touch them. By faith they passed through the Red Sea as by dry land, whereas the Egyptians, attempting to do so, were drowned. By faith the walls of Jericho fell down after they were encircled for seven days. By faith the harlot Rahab did not perish with those who did not believe, when she had received the spies with peace.

These Old Testament Saints became heroes by using their faith to achieve great acts.

In like manner, we can use our Faith to accomplish great things for the Lord. We all need to regain the excitement of the life which we have in Jesus Christ. We must also be encouraged to aggressively resist the debilitating effect which the systems of this world can have on our faith.

REPLACING DOUBT WITH REAL FAITH

I would like to remind you of the quality of faith that is able to activate divine virtue and direct God's attention towards our lives.

It may be correct to say that there are times when circumstances of life press us to be consumed by thoughts of worry and doubt. It is also correct to say that it is impossible to become excited about something when there is doubt in our minds. Let us take another look at what the scripture says about doubt and faith so that we can be assured of victory in every aspect of our walk with Christ.

James 1:5-8 New King James:

If any of you lacks wisdom, let him ask of God, who gives to all liberally and without reproach, and it will be given to him. But let him ask in faith, with no doubting, for he who doubts is like a wave of the sea driven and tossed by the wind. For let not that man supposes that he will receive anything from the Lord; he is a double-minded man, unstable in all his ways.

The principle to observe here is that 'faith activates the hand of God while doubt causes our path to become unstable and robs us of divine blessings.'

There can be no excitement in instability and depravity, but those who are full of faith will rejoice in the provisions of the Lord. James reminds us that there is an abundant supply available to meet our needs. The promise is that God will give liberally to all who ask in faith. This is a season for all saints to upgrade the level of faith that resides within. As we press towards the acquisition of our own facility, let us actively work on removing doubt, and replacing it with real faith in God's ability to give liberally.

There is a very good example of faith at work in the account of the woman with the issue of blood.

Mark 5:25-34

Now a certain woman had a flow of blood for twelve years, and had suffered many things from many physicians. She had spent all that she had and was no better, but rather grew worse. When she heard about Jesus, she came behind Him in the crowd and touched

His garment. For she said, "If only I may touch His clothes, I shall be made well." Immediately the fountain of her blood was dried up, and she felt in her body that she was healed of the affliction. And Jesus, immediately knowing in Himself that power had gone out of Him, turned around in the crowd and said, "Who touched My clothes?" But His disciples said to Him, "You see the multitude thronging You, and You say, 'Who touched Me?'" And He looked around to see her who had done this thing. But the woman, fearing and trembling, knowing what had happened to her, came and fell down before Him and told Him the whole truth. And He said to her, "Daughter, your faith has made you well. Go in peace, and be healed of your affliction."

REMOVE DOUBT AND EXCUSES:

This woman could have held on to many excuses based on the harsh reality of her life. These excuses would have created doubt and thereby deprived her of obtaining the healing which she pursued for many years.

She Suffered Long.

She could have focused on the variety of things which she had suffered at the hands of many physicians over the past 12 years. We must bear in mind that the practice of physicians in that day was not as refined nor were their approaches to medicine based on proven scientific observation as it is today.

She Would Have Been Considered Unclean.

Her condition would have rendered her unclean. She could have used that as an excuse not to pursue her healing among the crowd which followed Jesus.

She Would Have Been Weak.

She had opportunity to consider the physical weakness of her own body brought about by this prolong period of illness. This condition might have caused many to doubt their ability to press through that crowd in an attempt to obtain healing.

SHE GREW WORSE OVER TIME.
In spite of her persistent efforts and financial losses, she grew worse over time.

POSSESS REAL FAITH:
Notwithstanding the overwhelming negative circumstances of her life, this woman chose to exercise real faith in Christ Jesus to provide her healing. Her faith was so real; she did not require a face-to-face encounter with Him. In her mind she resolved, 'If I could only touch the hem of His garment, I know I will be made whole.' This faith was the key that unlocked the healing virtues of Christ in her life.

REAL FAITH RELEASES DIVINE VIRTUE:
I believe that there were many needs present among the crowd of people surrounding Jesus at that moment. There were those who simply desired to be present to see the miracles which He did. There were those who were pressing to engage His attention, as well as those who protected Him from the press of the crowd. In the midst of all this activity, the one thing that caught the attention of Christ was that one slight touch of real faith. This slight touch of faith was enough to release divine healing for this woman.

REAL FAITH COMMANDS THE ATTENTION OF CHRIST:
The response of Jesus assures us that He is hardwired to the frequency of 'real faith.' Every time we act in faith, He is alerted and responds favourably to our prayers. This woman did not have the privilege of conversing face to face with Jesus. She simply struggled to touch His garment from behind, yet Jesus knew that virtue had left Him. This quality of faith caused Jesus to turn around, (temporarily suspending His forward advance) to enquire and to declare a complete blessing on the woman.

Let us therefore work on eliminating doubt and worry from within us and replace them with real active faith. There is an abundant supply available for those who act in faith. Remember that without faith it is impossible to please Him.

Let's check our Understanding of the Chapter 6 - Heroes of Faith

1. What are some of the great feats achieved by the patriarchs? How?

2. Do you believe we too have the capacity to experience the level of accomplishments as did the Old Testament Saints? Why or Why not?

3. How does the systems of this world affect our Faith?

4. When can we be assured of God's divine blessings and our path to be stable & enjoyable?

5. Just as the woman with the issue of blood had to overcome, what are some of the doubts and excuses that you have in your mind when it comes to exercising Faith?

6. What happens when we exercise real faith?

CHAPTER SEVEN
ANOTHER LOOK AT FAITH

THE SCRIPTURES SAYS, WHEN MOSES CAME TO YEARS, HE REFUSED TO BE CALLED THE son of Pharaoh's Daughter. Hebrews 11:24

This was an actual outcome of spiritual and mental development. For forty years, he believed and lived a lie that he was the son of Pharaoh's Daughter. When he came to years, he found fault with what he once thought, believed and lived. The Church is coming to years in this era, that is, she is about entering an era of spiritual and mental development which will change the way we think, believe and operate. The 21st century Church will not look like the church of any other Christian era; this third day church will embody a degree of development and maturity which no other generation of believers have ever had. In this era, our ways of thinking and doing things will soon be challenged.

Faith *IS* the *SUBSTANCE* of things hoped for the *EVIDENCE* of things not seen [you do not need faith for what you already have or achieved] It is similar to your testimony and your potential [God is more interested in your *POTENTIAL* than your testimony] Potential speaks to what you can become or what you can accomplish, while a testimony speaks to what you have already done. That is why it is so ridiculous to hear people keep boasting on what they have done. It's done so move on to the next project – do not live on yesterday's feats...

SUBSTANCE:

Sub´stans (שׁוּכר, *rᵉkhūsh*; υπόστασις, *hupóstasis*): Lit. that which stands under, is in the Bible used chiefly of material goods and possessions. In the Old Testament it is the translation of numerous Hebrew words, of which *rᵉkhūsh*, "that which is gathered together," is one of the earliest and most significant (Genesis 12:5; Genesis 13:6; Genesis 15:14; 1Chronicles 27:31; Ezra 8:21, etc.). In the New Testament "substance" appears in a few passages as the translation of *ousía*, "being," "subsistence" (Luke 15:13), *húparxis*, "goods," "property" (Hebrews 10:34), *hupárchonta*, "things at hand" (Luke 8:3).

Faith is the SUBSTANCE = In a general sense, being something existing by itself; that which really is or exists; equally applicable to matter or spirit.

- Faith is like the soul of man, which is referred to as an immaterial substance, it is a substance endued with thought. We say a stone is a hard substance; a pillow is a soft substance.
- That which subsists by itself is called substance.
- The essential part; the main or material part. For example, we have the substance of the whole book.
- Something real, not imaginary; something solid, not empty.
- Goods; estate; means of living. Job's substance was seven thousand sheep, three thousand camels, Job 1.

THE EVIDENCE:

The Greek word denotes "putting to the test," examining for the purpose of proof, bringing to conviction. Thus if "test" or "proving" be adopted, a firm *conviction* of the reality of things not seen is implied as the result of putting to the proof.

It is important to note the true nature of faith according to the correct translation of Hebrews 11:1, as being the well-grounded and assured *conviction* of things not seen.

ALSO REMEMBER THAT IT IS THE TRIAL OF OUR FAITH THAT WORKS PATIENCE IN US:

PATIENCE:
"Patience" implies suffering, enduring or waiting, **as a determination of the will and not simply under necessity**. As such it is an essential Christian virtue to the exercise of which there are many exhortations.
James 1:2-3

My brothers, count it all joy when you fall into different kinds of temptations, knowing that the trying of your faith works patience.

We need to "wait patiently" for God, to endure uncomplainingly the various forms of sufferings, wrongs and evils that we meet with, and to patiently bear injustices which we cannot remedy and provocations we cannot remove.

Comes from a Latin or Greek patientia, from patior, to suffer.

The suffering of afflictions, pain, toil, calamity, provocation or other evil, with a calm, unruffled temper; endurance without murmuring or fretfulness.

Patience may spring from constitutional fortitude, from a kind of heroic pride, or from Christian submission to the divine will.

A calm temper which bears evils without murmuring or discontent.

The act or quality of waiting long for justice or expected good without discontent.

Have patience with me, and I will pay thee all. Matthew 18:21-26.

Perseverance; constancy in labour or exertion.

The quality of bearing offenses and injuries without anger or revenge.

Patience is often hard to gain and to maintain, but, in Romans 15:5, God is called "the God of patience" (the American Revised Version margin "steadfastness") as being able to grant that grace to those who look to Him and depend on Him for it.

It is in reliance on God and acceptance of His will, with trust in His goodness, wisdom and faithfulness, that we are enabled to endure and to hope steadfastly.

Patience should be allowed to have its perfect work James 1:4

But let patience have its perfect work, that you may be perfect and complete, lacking nothing.

When that happens it PRODUCES
Experience Romans 5:1-4
Hope Romans 15:1-4;
Romans 5:1-4

Therefore, having been justified by faith, we have peace with God through our Lord Jesus Christ, through whom also we have access by faith into this grace in which we stand, and rejoice in hope of the glory of God. And not only that, but we also glory in tribulations, knowing that tribulation produces perseverance; and perseverance, character; and character, hope.

Romans 15:1-4

We then who are strong ought to bear with the scruples of the weak, and not to please ourselves. Let each of us please his neighbor for his good, leading to edification. For even Christ did not please Himself; but as it is written, "The reproaches of those who reproached You fell on Me." For whatever things were written before were written for our learning, that we through the patience and comfort of the Scriptures might have hope.

Suffering with, for well-doing, is acceptable with God 1 Peter 2:20

For what credit is it if, when you are beaten for your faults, you take it patiently? But when you do good and suffer, if you take it patiently, this is commendable before God.

PATIENCE IS TO BE EXERCISED

    Running the race set before us Hebrews 12:1
    Bringing forth fruits Luke 8:15
    Well-doing Romans 2:7; Galatians 6:9
    Bearing the yoke Lamentations 3:27
    Tribulation Luke 21:19; Romans 12:12
    It is Necessary to the inheritance of the promises Hebrews 6:12; Hebrews 10:36

SHOULD BE ACCOMPANIED BY

Godliness 2 Peter 1:6 Faith 2 Thessolians 1:4; Hebrews 6:12; Revelation 13:10

Temperance 2 Peter 1:6 Long-suffering Colossians 1:11

Joyfulness Colossians 1:11

Exemplified

Job Job 1:21; James 5:11 Simeon Luke 2:25; Paul 2 Timothy 3:10

Abraham Hebrews 6:15 Prophets James 5:10 John Revelation 1:9

When PATIENCE is complete then we become entire lacking nothing...

Before we go into the next chapter, permit me to share a personal testimony here:

Over the past few years the Lord has been teaching me both sides to faith in Him.

While for most of us we only believe that faith is used to acquire what we deem to be the best from God. In light of that all we see is a gospel of prosperity, good, favourable and to be always happy. However, God has been allowing me to walk a dimension of this journey where I am learning that Faith's power is to enable those to suffer what otherwise they could not have suffered.

He has been teaching and revealing to me these both dimensions out of the book of Hebrew especially chapter 11. We all know how chapter 11 begins, with "Now faith is the substance of things hoped for... and then goes on to show what some of the brethren accomplished through faith and the record begins with those who did and accomplished some mighty feats of breakthrough and success. However, it then goes on to show what some of the others did through that same faith, here is an account: Hebrews 11:35b-38a

> *Others were tortured, not accepting deliverance, that they might obtain a better resurrection. Still others had trial of mockings and scourgings, yes, and of chains and imprisonment. They were stoned, they were sawn in two, were tempted, were slain with the sword. They wandered about in sheepskins and goatskins, being destitute, afflicted, tormented— of whom the world was not worthy. They wandered in deserts and mountains, in dens and caves of the earth.*

So, both of these experiences revealed the depth of faith these early Brethren had in God. You see living here in North America if we are not careful we might never be able to understand the depth of faith in God and when any form of pressure or trial comes we end up fainting, not realizing that the trial was allowed to test our faith in God. To build STRONG FAITH in us, but instead we for the most part end up failing that test.

Within the past few years I am being taught how to have my faith truly strengthened. I believe that I have passed quite a few dimensions of those tests and am looking forward with great hope to be able to pass the ones I am currently going through and those yet to come. And that God would truly find me faithful regardless to the level of tests that I may have to walk though.

My hope in writing this is that some of you may be blessed and encouraged and to understand what you may have been experiencing.

In our next chapter we want to explore Jesus Christ as being the centrality of our faith.

Chapter Seven: Another Look At Faith

Let's check our Understanding of the Chapter 7 – Another Look at Faith

1. How does Moses' refusal to be called the son of Pharaoh's Daughter relate to what is to take place and/or already taking place in the 21st Century Church?

2. Can you describe what Faith is in your own words? What do you need Faith for?

3. What does the Hebrew word *"rᵉkhūsh"* translated substance in the Old Testament mean?

4. What are the Greek words translated substance in the New Testament and what does each of them mean?

5. How will you then explain the phrase *"Faith is the SUBSTANCE"?*

6. The Greek word translated Evidence denotes _____

7. What is your understanding of the true nature of faith based on the accurate translation of Hebrews 11:1?

8. What are the Latin and Greek words translated 'patience'? What do they mean?

9. Do you believe this is an important virtue in a Christian's life? Why or why not?

10. What are some of the ways that patience can spring forth from?

11. It is in _____ on God and _____ of His will, with _____ in His goodness, wisdom and faithfulness, that we are _____ to _____ and to hope steadfastly.

12. Why should we desire to acquire patience in our lives …. What does it produce?

13. How are we to exercise patience in our lives?

14. What are the other characteristics that should accompany patience in-order for us to obtain the inheritance of the promises?

15. Can you think of any biblical examples of those who inherited promises through great faith and patience?

CHAPTER EIGHT
JESUS CHRIST – THE CENTRALITY OF OUR FAITH

1 CORINTHIANS 1:17-24

> *For Christ did not send me to baptize, but to preach the gospel; not in wisdom of words, lest the cross of Christ should be made of no effect. For the preaching of the cross is foolishness to those being lost, but to us being saved, it is the power of God. For it is written, "I will destroy the wisdom of the wise, and I will set aside the understanding of the perceiving ones." Where is the wise? Where is the scribe? Where is the lawyer of this world? Has not God made foolish the wisdom of this world? For since, in the wisdom of God, the world by wisdom did not know God, it pleased God by the foolishness of preaching to save those who believe. For the Jews ask for a sign, and the Greeks seek after wisdom; but we preach Christ crucified, to the Jews a stumbling block, and to the Greeks foolishness. But to them, the called-out ones, both Jews and Greeks, Christ is the power of God and the wisdom of God.*

In this chapter, I would like to address the importance for us to keep Jesus Christ and the finished work of Calvary as the central focus of our lives as Born-Again Believers/Disciples.

There are still those who are adding and subtracting from the pure message of the gospel of Jesus Christ and in doing so they are preaching another Jesus and another gospel. Let me take the time to explain what I am talking about.

The Apostle Paul who was a Pharisee who accepted Jesus Christ as his personal Lord and Saviour, thereby converting from Judaism, wrote the following passages of Scripture:

Philippians 3:1-21

And that's about it, friends. Be glad in God! I don't mind repeating what I have written in earlier letters, and I hope you don't mind hearing it again. Better safe than sorry--so here goes. Steer clear of the barking dogs, those religious busybodies, all bark and no bite. All they're interested in is appearances--knife-happy circumcisers, I call them. The real believers are the ones the Spirit of God leads to work away at this ministry, filling the air with Christ's praise as we do it. We couldn't carry this off by our own efforts, and we know it--even though we can list what many might think are impressive credentials. You know my pedigree: a legitimate birth, circumcised on the eighth day; an Israelite from the elite tribe of Benjamin; a strict and devout adherent to God's law; a fiery defender of the purity of my religion, even to the point of persecuting Christians; a meticulous observer of everything set down in God's law Book. The very credentials these people are waving around as something special, I'm tearing up and throwing out with the trash--along with everything else I used to take credit for. And why? Because of Christ. Yes, all the things I once thought were so important are gone from my life. Compared to the high privilege of knowing Christ Jesus as my Master, firsthand, everything I once thought I had going for me is insignificant--dog dung. I've dumped it all in the trash so that I could embrace Christ and be embraced by him. I didn't want some petty, inferior brand of righteousness that comes from keeping a list of rules when I could get the robust kind that comes from trusting Christ--God's righteousness. I gave up all that inferior stuff so I could know Christ personally, experience his resurrection power, be a partner in his suffering, and go all the way with him to death itself. If there was any way to get in on the resurrection from the dead, I wanted to do it. I'm not saying that I have this all together, that I have it made. But I am well on my way, reaching out for Christ, who has so wondrously reached out for me. Friends, don't get me wrong: By no means do I count myself an expert in all of this, but I've got my eye on the goal, where God is beckoning us onward--to Jesus. I'm off and running, and I'm not turning back. So let's keep focused on that goal, those of us who want everything God has for us. If any of you have something else in mind, something less than total commitment, God will clear your blurred vision--you'll see it yet! Now that we're on the right track, let's stay on it. Stick with me, friends. Keep track of those you see running this same course, headed for this same goal. There are many out there taking other paths, choosing other goals, and trying to get you to go along with them. I've warned you of them many times; sadly, I'm having to do it again. All they want is easy street. They hate Christ's Cross. But easy street is a dead-end street. Those who live there make their bellies their gods; belches are their praise; all they can think of is their appetites. But there's far more to life for us. We're citizens of high heaven! We're waiting the arrival of the Savior, the Master, Jesus Christ, who will transform our earthy bodies into glorious bodies like his own. He'll make us beautiful and whole with the same powerful skill by which he is putting everything as it should be, under and around him.

In Galatians Chapter 3 once again the Apostle Paul had to address some very pertinent issues regarding the Faith.

QUESTIONS FOR THE GALATIANS
Galatians 3:1-5

You foolish Galatians, who has bewitched you, before whose eyes Jesus Christ was publicly portrayed as crucified? This is the only thing I want to find out from you: did you receive the Spirit by the works of the Law, or by hearing with faith? Are you so foolish? Having begun by the Spirit, are you now being perfected by the flesh? Did you suffer so many things in vain — if indeed it was in vain? So then, does He who provides you with the Spirit and works miracles among you, do it by the works of the Law, or by hearing with faith?

RIGHTEOUSNESS BY FAITH
Even so Abraham BELIEVED GOD, AND IT WAS RECKONED TO HIM AS RIGHTEOUSNESS. Therefore, be sure that it is those who are of faith who are sons of Abraham. The Scripture, foreseeing that God would justify the Gentiles by faith, preached the gospel beforehand to Abraham, saying, "ALL THE NATIONS WILL BE BLESSED IN YOU." So then those who are of faith are blessed with Abraham, the believer. For as many as are of the works of the Law are under a curse; for it is written, "CURSED IS EVERYONE WHO DOES NOT ABIDE BY ALL THINGS WRITTEN IN THE BOOK OF THE LAW, TO PERFORM THEM." Now that no one is justified by the Law before God is evident; for, "THE RIGHTEOUS MAN SHALL LIVE BY FAITH." However, the Law is not of faith; on the contrary, "HE WHO PRACTICES THEM SHALL LIVE BY THEM." Christ redeemed us from the curse of the Law, having become a curse for us—for it is written, "CURSED IS EVERYONE WHO HANGS ON A TREE"— in order that in Christ Jesus the blessing of Abraham might come to the Gentiles, so that we would receive the promise of the Spirit through faith.

FAITH VERSUS THE LAW
Galatians 3:15-29

> *Brethren, I speak in terms of human relations: even though it is only a man's covenant, yet when it has been ratified, no one sets it aside or adds conditions to it. Now the promises were spoken to Abraham and to his seed. He does not say, "And to seeds," as referring to many, but rather to one, "And to your seed," that is, Christ. What I am saying is this: The Law, which came four hundred and thirty years later, does not invalidate a covenant previously ratified by God, so as to nullify the promise. For if the inheritance is based on law, it is no longer based on a promise; but God has granted it to Abraham by means of a promise. Why the Law then? It was added because of transgressions, having been ordained through angels by the agency of a mediator, until the seed would come to whom the promise had been made. Now a mediator is not for one party only; whereas God*

is only one. Is the Law then contrary to the promises of God? May it never be! For if a law had been given which was able to impart life, then righteousness would indeed have been based on law. But the Scripture has shut up everyone under sin, so that the promise by faith in Jesus Christ might be given to those who believe. But before faith came, we were kept in custody under the law, being shut up to the faith which was later to be revealed. Therefore the Law has become our tutor to lead us to Christ, so that we may be justified by faith. But now that faith has come, we are no longer under a tutor. For you are all sons of God through faith in Christ Jesus. For all of you who were baptized into Christ have clothed yourselves with Christ. There is neither Jew nor Greek, there is neither slave nor free man, there is neither male nor female; for you are all one in Christ Jesus. And if you belong to Christ, then you are Abraham's descendants, heirs according to promise.

QUESTIONS FOR THE GALATIANS

After giving such a great exhortation of what happens to a Believer when he had believed; Apostle Paul then begins the body or bulk of his letter with a pretty nasty comment: "You foolish Galatians, who has bewitched you"? What were you thinking did someone cast a spell on you or something; is the real point here that Paul is trying to get across. For while Apostle Paul was with them he painted them a picture of what the crucifixion of Jesus was like to the point that they could see it like they were there. The word there actually means to post it a sign. Therefore, how could the Galatians not be able to discern between the teachings of Christ and the teachings of the Judaizers. Hence this is why he calls them foolish.

Now after that rebuke Paul asks them a series of questions that are very important and are pretty much the basis for the rest of this letter:

1. Did you receive the Spirit by the works of the Law, or by hearing with faith?
2. Are you so foolish? Having begun by the Spirit, are you now being perfected by the flesh?
3. Did you suffer so many things in vain— if indeed it was in vain?

4. So then, does He who provides you with the Spirit and works miracles among you, do it by the works of the Law, or by hearing with faith?

Looking at these questions we can clearly see that Apostle Paul is drawing a contrast between the works of the Spirit and the works of the flesh. Look at some of the contrasts here that he is drawing:

- Hearing with faith versus works
- Being perfected in the Spirit versus being perfected by doing good things
- God working miracles by the Spirit versus by doing the works of the Law
- Apostle Paul here is trying to imply: "look your salvation is of a spiritual nature and not of a human nature. You cannot add anything to the work of the Spirit. It is by faith."

RIGHTEOUSNESS BY FAITH

The obvious answer to all of Apostle Paul's questions is an emphatic, No! He then goes on to state: "Even so Abraham BELIEVED GOD, AND IT WAS RECKONED TO HIM AS RIGHTEOUSNESS." I love this verse. Abraham lived before Moses and before the Law was given; so in that time, being in right standing with God was based on him [Abraham having faith] believing in God and His promises. What a simple faith! God would speak and Abraham would believe; I could write an entire, separate book on this, but I won't.

Now Apostle Paul goes on to say something that is great for us: Therefore, be sure that it is those who are of faith who are sons of Abraham. The Scripture, foreseeing that God would justify the Gentiles by faith, preached the gospel beforehand to Abraham, saying, "ALL THE NATIONS WILL BE BLESSED IN YOU." The Gentiles who would believe are part of that promise for all nations would be blessed through the faith of Abraham. Because of Abraham's obedience to the word of God we can now become sons of Abraham and partakers of the same blessings that he received, but now I am jumping ahead of Apostle Paul; so let's back track here. Abraham believes God and he was made right with God and everyone who believes like Abraham would become the sons of Abraham.

This is how all nations will be blessed in Abraham. So then those who are of faith are blessed with Abraham. Amen?

Apostle Paul, however, makes a slight shift for the understanding of the Galatians and states: "For as many as are of the works of the Law are under a curse; for it is written, "CURSED IS EVERYONE WHO DOES NOT ABIDE BY ALL THINGS WRITTEN IN THE BOOK OF THE LAW, TO PERFORM THEM." Here the Apostle Paul does a masterful job in building an argument against what the "Judaizers" were preaching, and we must remember that. He shows that if the Law is not fully obeyed there is not a blessing but a curse for those people. Therefore we must see that no one is justified by the Law before God but that the Righteous man shall live by faith. Being though that the law is not based on faith but on the doing the works of the law. Therefore Christ redeemed us from the curse of the Law, having become a curse for us—for it is written, "CURSED IS EVERYONE WHO HANGS ON A TREE"— in order that in Christ Jesus the blessing of Abraham might come to the Gentiles. Now because of the work of Jesus on the cross we can have the blessing of Abraham which is righteousness through faith.

Now what is all this meaning for the Galatians and for us today? The Galatians were being faced with the Judaizers; saying you must keep the law and all its commandments in addition to believing Christ. Apostle Paul's response to that was a flat no; that is not the case because if you want to add the Law then you have to keep all the Law and no one can do that. Therefore our salvation is based on Christ alone and through believing in Christ alone we can have the blessing that Abraham had; righteousness through faith and being called a friend of God. Remember that Abraham was the friend of God. Now through the sacrifice of Jesus we can also be called the friends of God.

Now the Spirit is the guarantee of all this so Apostle Paul says we would receive the promise of the Spirit through faith. Here Apostle Paul harkens back to his questions of the contrasting of the Spirit versus the flesh. Above we see how he shows that the work of Christ is the work of Spirit in our lives. As Christ died to the Law so we die to the Law so we don't have to obey it anymore. We cannot go back. We are not to go back. We have died to this. We, now through faith have the Spirit and as such flesh cannot glory in the work of the Spirit. None! The work of the Spirit is the work of God in our life.

The Apostle Paul goes further by belabouring this point by illustrating this even more: "Dear brothers and sisters, here's an example from everyday life. Just as no one can set aside or amend an irrevocable agreement, so it is in this case. Now the promises were spoken to Abraham and to his seed. He does not say, "And to seeds," as referring to many, but rather to one, "And to your seed," that is, Christ." Apostle Paul states that the promise made to Abraham about his seed was about Christ and was not for the nation of Israel. Now Paul is going to begin to explain why the Law was given: This is what I am trying to say: The agreement God made with Abraham could not be cancelled 430 years later when God gave the Law to Moses. God would be breaking His promise. For if the inheritance could be received only by keeping the Law; then it would not be the result of accepting God's promise. But God gave it to Abraham as a promise. Well then, why was the Law given? It was given to show people how guilty they are. The Law shows us that we are sinners. If it was not for the Law, then we would not know our sin. If you look at the 10 Commandments then you can see how guilty we stand before God. Clearly something needed to be done and what was done was God gave His Son Jesus as a sacrifice for us so that by believing in Him we would not have to pay the penalty of death.

The Scriptures have declared that we are all prisoners of sin, so the only way to receive God's promise is to believe in Jesus Christ. Until faith in Christ was shown to us as the way of becoming right with God, we were guarded by the Law. We were kept in protective custody, so to speak, until we could put our faith in the coming Saviour. Let me put it another way. The Law was our guardian and teacher to lead us until Christ came. So now, through faith in Christ, we are made right with God.

The Law showed us our sin as a schoolteacher shows us the right way to do things in math and science. The Law was put as our guardian until Christ came. The Law watched over us and kept us in check until the Lord provided salvation from our sins. The Law can be summed up in this way, "do this and you shall do good and you and I (being God) can live in harmony." Now that Christ has come, we no longer need to strive after the works of the flesh to be made right in the sight of God just believe and trust in Christ and then we can be made right through the gift of the Holy Spirit.

Galatians 3:26-28

For you are all sons of God through faith in Christ Jesus. For all of you who were baptized into Christ have clothed yourselves with Christ. There is neither Jew nor Greek, there is neither slave nor free man, there is neither male nor female; for you are all one in Christ Jesus. And if you belong to Christ, then you are Abraham's descendants, heirs according to promise.

Now through Christ we have become sons of God and heirs according to the promise of Abraham. We who have been baptized into Christ that is water baptized have clothed ourselves with Christ. That means that we have symbolically put on Christ and it is no longer us. This harkens to the language of Romans when Paul talks about baptism in the sense that we die with Christ when are baptized and we are raised with Him to new life. It is amazing that Christ so longs to be unified with us. We now experience union with God and with Christ through the blessing of Abraham and baptism of Christ.

CONCLUSION
Apostle Paul laid out a great theological foundation of the blessings of salvation and being made righteous through faith. We can clearly see that the father of our Faith, Abraham played a great role and we can learn from his obedience to God that we to can be made righteous in the same way by believing in Christ. Through believing in Christ now we have the blessings of eternal life and there is no longer a striving for the work after the flesh but after the Spirit.

In our next chapter we will look at our ever-increasing faith.

Let's check our Understanding of the Chapter 8: Jesus Christ – The Centrality of Our Faith

1. Do you agree with the author's statement "There are still those who are adding and subtracting from the pure message of the gospel of Jesus Christ and in doing so they are preaching another Jesus and another gospel." Explain.

2. Why is it important for us to keep Jesus Christ and the finished work of Calvary as the central focus of our lives as Born-Again Believers?

3. What was Apostle Paul's exhortation to the Galatians on this issue have to say about his painstaking efforts to portray Jesus Christ in their midst?

4. Is it possible for a believer to become righteous? If so, how?

5. According to Galatians 3:15-29 what is our inheritance in God based upon?

6. In-order to receive our inheritance what is it that we need to have? How are we to obtain it?

7. What was the significance of Apostle Paul's series of questions to the Galatians?

8. When God spoke to Abraham and promised to bless and increase his seed, who was He referring to?

9. What was the purpose of the law?

10. Do we have to go back to keeping the law in-order to become Abraham's descendants?

11. How can we be justified before God?

12. As Apostle Paul explains to the Galatians, why was the "Judiazers" preaching false/in-accurate?

13. Do you believe there is any requirement for us to keep the Law and all of its commandments in addition to believing Christ?

14. Do you believe we too can be friends of God just as Abraham did? If so, how?

15. What did Jesus' sacrifice on the cross do for us?

CHAPTER NINE
Ever Increasing Faith

EVER-INCREASING FAITH
ROMANS 1:17

> *For in it the righteousness of God is revealed from faith to faith; as it is written, "The just shall live by faith.* [Emphasis Author's]

2 Corinthians 3:18

> *But we all, with unveiled face, beholding as in a mirror the glory of the Lord, are being transformed into the same image from glory to glory, just as by the Spirit of the Lord.*

As we continue we need to remind ourselves that God is looking for a generation of people that would be a true representation of His glory in the earth. God is seeking for a generation with a Kingdom mindset/lifestyle, not just salvation. That is a Kingdom generation.

The Moses generation possessed a salvation mindset, they were saved and delivered from the hands of the Egyptians (they possessed "first level faith"), however they neither possessed the mentality nor the lifestyle required to step into God's promises, not possessions. (Life does not consist in the abundance of things we possess Luke 12:15). They all died in the wilderness except Joshua and Caleb who had a different mentality

– Numbers 14:24 (Numbers 13 dealing with the spies who went to spy out the land).

The "Joshua/Caleb Generation" possessed the dimensions of an ever-increasing faith, they walked in three realms of faith - foundational, possessing and finishing faith, they possessed the right mindset, the kingdom mindset that allowed them to inherit the promise, to obtain the inheritance.

The Hebrew ("aman") and the Greek ("pistis") are words for "FAITH" and they convey the meaning: that which is certain or sure, it is also translated verily, truly or indeed!

How do we go from "Faith to Faith?" The Word of God declares: "So then faith comes by hearing, and hearing by the word of God." Romans 10:17-18. So then, Faith increases in direct proportion to the Word that we are receiving. If all we are receiving is a "Salvation Word" then that is where our faith will remain. So in essence our revelation base must increase for our faith to increase. This is why we must be in the Word and be connected to God-Ordained revelators of His Word. The more Christ is revealed in us and to us the greater our faith will become. The apostle Paul by the Holy Spirit brought this point home in a very profound and forceful manner:

Colossians 1:24-29

I now rejoice in my sufferings for you, and fill up in my flesh what is lacking in the afflictions of Christ, for the sake of His body, which is the church, of which I became a minister according to the stewardship from God which was given to me for you, to fulfill the word of God, the mystery which has been hidden from ages and from generations, but now has been revealed to His saints. To them God willed to make known what are the riches of the glory of this mystery among the Gentiles: which is Christ in you, the hope of glory. Him we preach, warning every man and teaching every man in all wisdom, that we may present every man perfect in Christ Jesus. To this end I also labour, striving according to His working which works in me mightily. [Emphasis Author's]

We are moving as it were on An Ever-Increasing Faith; from Faith for Salvation to Faith for Possessing our destiny and inheritance to Faith for finishing all that the Lord has assigned for us to accomplish.

Please note that the devil will have no greater joy than to see some who walked in great dimensions of faith to draw back and have their faith diminished. The writer of Hebrews declares: Hebrews 10:35-39

Therefore do not cast away your confidence, which has great reward. For you have need of endurance, so that after you have done the will of God, you may receive the promise: "For yet a little while, And He who is coming will come and will not tarry. Now the just shall live by faith; But if anyone draws back, My soul has no pleasure in him." But we are not of those who draw back to perdition, but of those who believe to the saving of the soul.

FOUNDATIONAL FAITH is found in Hebrews 11. It is vital and without option. It is man's faith in God. It is "first principles" faith-"faith toward (upon) God." It is INDIVIDUAL faith that meets our needs in five basic areas:

1. We are justified by faith (Romans 5:1).
2. Our hearts are circumcised in water baptism by faith (Colossians 2:11-12).
3. We are filled with the Holy Ghost by faith (Galatians 3:1-5).
4. We are healed by faith (1 Peter 2:24).
5. Our financial needs are met by faith (Philippians 4:19).

With regard to the latter, everyone is screaming and slobbering, "Money come to me!" However, someone needs to preach and practice "Money go through me!" God's wealth is wealth to be stewarded and redistributed. It is given to establish His covenant and to evangelize the nations (Deuteronomy 8:18 with Matthew 28:18-20; Mark 16:15-20; Acts 1:8).

FINISHING FAITH is found in Hebrews 12. Jesus Christ is the Author and the Finisher of our faith. Finishing faith is God's faith in Himself in and through a Corporate Man. This is the faith of God (Mark 11:22) for these times (Luke 18:1,8). This is faith for creation and for the nations.

This kind of FAITH has the ability to call into existence things that do not exist. – Romans 4:13-25 AWESOME! – FAITH THAT RECEIVES THE PROMISE!

WE NEED to possess this quality of FAITH to see Isaiah 54:1-2 become a reality in and through us – LENGTHEN your cords and STRENGTHEN your staves! – INCREASE WILL COME!!!

Be encouraged! The One who brought us out will bring us in (Deuteronomy 6:23 with Psalm 138:8; Jeremiah 29:11; Philippians 1:6).

"The hands of Zerubbabel (a type of Jesus the Messiah) have laid the foundation of this house; his hands shall also finish it..." (Zechariah 4:9).

In our following chapter, we would like to look at Faith/Belief.

Let's check our Understanding of the Chapter 9: Ever Increasing Faith

1. What type of present-day generation is God seeking to have upon this earth?

2. Can you differentiate between the mindset we are expected to have today and that of Moses' generation?

3. Who were the 2 survivors from the Moses generation to have entered the promise land?

4. Why were the Moses generation unable to step into the promises God had made to their forefathers?

5. What difference was seen in the mindset of the Joshua/Caleb generation that allowed them to inherit the promise?

6. What are the Hebrew and Greek words translated "FAITH"? What meaning do these words convey?

7. Do you believe it is possible for us to go from faith to faith? If so, how can we do that?

8. The author declares "our revelation base must increase for our faith to increase. This is why we must be in the Word and be connected to God-Ordained revelators of His Word." Do you agree? Explain.

9. According to Apostle Paul, what is the mystery revealed to us His church which was hidden from the previous generations?

10. Will you agree that we are on a journey of Ever-Increasing Faith? Why?

11. Which 5 areas of needs are met by individual faith? Support your response with scriptural references.

12. Which Scriptures talk to the fact that wealth poured into the hands of his senate the Church is for the purpose of establishing His covenant and evangelizing the nations?

13. What kind of Faith would enable us to call into existence things that do not exist?

14. Why do we need to have this type of Faith? What are we to accomplish with this type of Faith?

15. Is it possible for us to attain this type of Faith?

Chapter Ten
Faith/Believe

But the just shall live by his faith (Habakkuk 2:4; compare Romans 1:17; Galatians 3:11; Hebrews 10:38).

One quickly learns from the Bible that faith is a vital key to this walk with God. The writer of Hebrews states that "without Faith it is impossible to please God" (Hebrews 11:6). Abraham became a partaker of the covenant by faith (Genesis 15:6). And faith must operate from the beginning (Romans 5:1,2) to the end of this walk (1 Peter 1:9; Hebrews 12:2; 2 Corinthians 5:7).

In Hebrew, the word "faith," or its verb "believe" (Strong's #539, AMAN), means to build up or support, foster or nurse (as parent), to render firm, be permanent, make secure, trust, be true, make expert, establish, take the right-hand way, and Amen. The Greek word (PISTIS, Strong's #4102) conveys convincing by evidence, to pacify, assent, reliance, constancy, truth and trust. The Bible reveals the following:

1. Faith is a gift of God: 1 Corinthians 12:9; Romans 12:3; Ephesians 2:8.
2. Faith is sent by God's word to those who hear: Romans 10:17; Proverbs 20:12.
3. Only God's faith will accomplish the job: Mark 11:22; Romans 3:22; Revelation 14:12; Galatians 2:20.

4. One needs faith to please and come to God: Hebrews 11:6; Ephesians 3:12; Galatians 5:6.
5. Faith is necessary to be:
    a. justified – Romans 5:1; Galatians 2:16; 3:6-9,24
    b. healed – Matthew 9:22; Mark 5:34; Luke 8:48; 17:19; Acts 14:9
    c. sanctified – Acts 26:18
    d. purified – Acts 15:9
    e. saved – Ephesians 2:8; 2 Timothy 3:15; John 3:16; Acts 16:31
    f. established – Isaiah 7:9; 2 Chronicles 20:20; Colossians 2:7; Jude 20
6. Faith is reality – Hebrews 11:1
7. Faith operates by love – Galatians 5:6

1 John 5:4 declares:

For whatsoever is born of God overcometh the world; and this is the victory that overcometh the world, even our faith.

VICTORIES OF MEN AND WOMEN...
Hebrews 11 gives us many examples of men and women who had grown strong in their faith, and because of their faith lived victorious lives. In our study of Hebrews 11:32-35a we see the victories of faith.

And what more shall I say? For the time would fail me to tell of Gideon and Barak and Samson and Jephthah, also of David and Samuel and the prophets: who through faith subdued kingdoms, worked righteousness, obtained promises, stopped the mouths of lions, quenched the violence of fire, escaped the edge of the sword, out of weakness were made strong, became valiant in battle, turned to flight the armies of the aliens. Women received their dead raised to life again.

These Believers overcame every imaginable type of adversity through faith. Samson defeated 1,000 men; David killed Goliath, all because they trusted God.

The dominant thought in all these examples is triumph over adversity – victory and accomplishment in spite of trial. This is one great side to the experience of faith, but there is another—verses 35b-38 give the other side of the picture.

> *Others were tortured, not accepting deliverance, that they might obtain a better resurrection. Still others had trial of mockings and scourgings, yes, and of chains and imprisonment. They were stoned, they were sawn in two, were tempted, were slain with the sword. They wandered about in sheepskins and goatskins, being destitute, afflicted, tormented—of whom the world was not worthy. They wandered in deserts and mountains, in dens and caves of the earth.*

The rapid transition to the thought of unrelieved suffering is very effective.

Faith is not always rewarded in this life. In my opinion, this is an even greater manifestation of the power of faith.

Faith's power is to enable those to suffer what otherwise they could not have suffered.

Here is a group of people that didn't gain great victories out on the battlefield. They didn't perform great feats for God, but in my opinion, these are the real heroes. They trusted God when the day was dark, when the night was long, the suffering was great, and when there was no deliverance for them at all: WOW!!!

Hebrews 11:35

> *Women received their dead raised to life again. And* <u>others were tortured</u>, *not accepting deliverance, that they might obtain* a better resurrection. [Emphasis Author's]

Notice the transition in this verse, *"Women received their dead raise to life again* **– and others were tortured."** The transition is startling, from victory to torture.

That word "tortured" is from the Greek word *tumpanizo*, which means: **"to torture with the tympanum"**.

This was a drum shaped instrument over which criminals were stretched and then beaten with clubs. The word means: "to be beat to death".

"*...not accepting **deliverance**....*" These people could have recanted their faith and denied God, and they would have been set free. But they chose torture over apostasy.

Do you see the relevance of this to the Hebrew Believers who were being tempted to apostatize or revolt from the faith and turn back to Old Covenant Judaism?

The text goes on to say, "*...**that they might obtain a better resurrection**"* – they refused to deny the Lord and accept release in order that they might obtain a better resurrection.

The reference to a "***better resurrection***" is in contrast to the raising of the first part of the verse – "*Women received their **dead raised to life again**:*"

The words, "***raised to life again***," are from the Greek word *anastasis*. It is the same word that is translated resurrection. The New American Standard puts it this way:

Hebrews 11:35 (NASB)

Women received back their dead by resurrection; *and others were tortured, not accepting their release, so that they might obtain a* better *resurrection;"* [Emphasis Author's]

How could anyone endure such torture when they could have escaped it? **By faith**, they believed God's promise of resurrection life. They were willing to die because physical death was not the end for them.

Today, when we think of the word "**martyr**", we often conjure up negative connotations in our minds.

For example, we may say to ourselves or out loud: "He or she has a martyr's complex." What we mean by that is that such a person seems preoccupied, even obsessed, with their own pain, suffering, hurt, or sickness for the purpose of getting other people to pity them, to feel sorry for them.

In other words, they use their real or imagined suffering and sickness by convincing themselves and others that they are such great people, because they are martyrs.

In the eyes of others, such "martyrs" seem overly self-centered, manipulative, and display hypochondriac **(the belief that you have some serious aliment)** behaviors. They become so focused on their situation that they blow it all out of proportion – thus making mountains out of molehills. That's one negative example of martyrs.

When it comes to true Christian martyrs, that's more difficult to talk about since it violates our comfort zones; stirs up guilt feelings; makes us ashamed of ourselves; and may even convict us of our sins.

I don't know if you're like me, but true, sincere Christian martyrs make me nervous! Why?

Well, whenever I read about true Christian martyrs and the stories of their martyrdom, I get nervous, because their lives, along with the circumstances surrounding their suffering and death, reveal to me how much more committed they were to Christ than I am.

These martyrs and their martyrdom stories bring me up short; and make me realize how I have failed miserably in so many circumstances to be the kind of Christian that they were; to do the Christ-like things that they did; to speak the Christ-like words that they spoke.

In short, these martyrs and their martyrdom convict me of my sin and tell me that I still have a lot of growing to do as a Follower of Christ.

Hebrews 11:36

Still others had trial of mockings and scourgings, yes, and of chains and imprisonment. [Emphasis Author's]

"Still others had trial of mockings"... The next time that we are mocked because of our faith, let's remember that this was the mildest form of suffering, which many who went before us were called upon to endure.

The sneers and unkind words of the world are not worthy of comparison with the pain, which other Believers have had to bear. It has always been the lot of God's servants to be derided, reproached, and insulted:

Galatians 4:29

But as then he that was born after the flesh persecuted him that was born after the Spirit, even so it is now.

Saints, could this be true? – If we are not being mocked, sneered at, scoffed at, it is because we are too lax in our ways, too quiet in our talk, or too worldly in our walk.

They also underwent ***"scourgings"*** – whipping; this was a common form of punishment and was usually inflicted before a martyr was put to death. Our Lord suffered this:
Matthew 27:26

Then released he Barabbas unto them: and when he had scourged Jesus, he delivered him to be crucified.

The Apostles suffered this also:
Acts 16:23

And when they had laid <u>many stripes</u> *upon them, they cast them into prison* [Emphasis Author's]

They also endured ***"chains and imprisonment"*** – this has been the experience of God's faithful witnesses in every generation.
2 Corinthians 11:23

Are they ministers of Christ? (I speak as a fool) I am more; in labours more abundant, in stripes above measure, <u>in prisons more frequent</u> [Emphasis Author's]

We need to understand that the prisons of those days were far different than the comfortable buildings in which criminals are now incarcerated. Look at:
Jeremiah 38:6

So they took Jeremiah and cast him into the dungeon *of Malchiah the king's son, which was in the court of the prison, and they let Jeremiah down with ropes. And in the dungeon there was no water, but mire. So Jeremiah sank in the mire.* [Emphasis Author's]

Jeremiah 38:11-13

So Ebed-Melech took the men with him and went into the house of the king under the treasury, and took from there old clothes and old rags, and let them down by ropes into the dungeon *to Jeremiah.*

Then Ebed-Melech the Ethiopian said to Jeremiah, "Please put these old clothes and rags under your armpits, under the ropes." And Jeremiah did so. So they pulled Jeremiah up with ropes and lifted him out of the dungeon. And Jeremiah remained in the court of the prison. [Emphasis Author's]

This gives us some idea of what prisons were like. Jeremiah was beaten and thrown in prison because he boldly declared the Word of the Lord.

God's children were thrown into dark and damp dungeons below the earth, unheated, unpaved, unilluminated, and with no bathrooms because of their testimony.

Paul and Silas were beaten and thrown in prison:
Acts 16:23-24

And when they had laid many stripes on them, they threw them into prison, commanding the jailer to keep them securely. Having received such a charge, he put them into the inner prison and fastened their feet in the stocks.

The writer of Hebrews goes on to say: Hebrews 11:37

They were stoned, *they were* sawn in two, *were* tempted, *were* slain with the sword. *They* wandered about *in sheepskins and goatskins, being* destitute, afflicted, tormented; [Emphasis Author's]

"They were stoned"... this was the fate of many of the Prophets. Jesus said in:
Matthew 23:37

O Jerusalem, Jerusalem, thou that killest the prophets, and <u>stonest them</u> *which are sent unto thee* [Emphasis Author's]

Stoning was the fate of Zechariah:
2 Chronicles 24:20-21

And the Spirit of God came upon Zechariah the son of Jehoiada the priest, which stood above the people, and said unto them, Thus saith

God, Why transgress ye the commandments of the LORD, that ye cannot prosper? because ye have forsaken the LORD, he hath also forsaken you. And they conspired against him, <u>*and stoned him with stones*</u> *at the commandment of the king in the court of the house of the LORD.* [Emphasis Author's]

Well, some would say that was Old Testament Saints. Then I would remind them of Stephen, the first New Testament martyr, who was stoned to death, and so was Apostle Paul, but Paul survived and continued to preach.

They also **"were sawn asunder"** there is no record in Scripture of anyone being put to death in this way, though tradition tells us that Isaiah's life was ended in this manner. That some of God's children perished in this way is clear from our text. Suetonius (the Roman historian) records that the emperor, Caligula, often condemned persons to be sawn through the middle.

They also **"were tempted!"**

The word "tempted", standing as it does between the more terrible physical sufferings of being stoned and sawn asunder, on the one hand, and slain with the sword on the other, has perplexed many, and some have tried to substitute some other word or remove it entirely from the text.

It is probably best to leave it as it is and suggest that one of the worst tortures was not that of the body but of the conscience; when the torturer would offer the victim opportunity to recant and thus obtain his freedom.

This would test their true priorities; were they spiritual or physical?

Or when they were tempted by those of their own household, who would beg them to denounce their faith and save their lives.

Or they might have been tempted to question God's goodness or justice. Yes, temptations can cause real sufferings.

They also **"were slain with the sword!"**

I want you to notice a contrast here. Back in verse 34 we have been told some through faith **"escaped the edge of the sword"**, but in verse 37 some through faith **"were slain with the sword"**.

Elijah escaped Jezebel's vengeance, but other Prophets of the Lord were slain with the sword at that time.

So too in the apostolic age, Herod Agrippa killed James, the brother of John, with the sword (Acts 12:2), but when he tried to do the same thing to Peter, Peter escaped.

By faith one lived, and by faith the other died. Are you seeing this?

So then, the question becomes—who decides who lives and who dies? And both will be in faith! You understanding this?

It's great to be able to get up and quote Scriptures such as: Psalms 34:7, 17 KJV

The angel of the LORD encampeth round about them that fear him, and delivereth them.... The righteous cry, and the LORD heareth, and delivereth them out of all their troubles.

That's wonderful, and God does that, but sometimes He chooses not to deliver the Believer from suffering.

God doesn't always raise a person up from a bed of sickness. While some are healed, there are thousands today who are in the hospitals, thousands lying on beds of pain.

<u>**Strong faith trusts God in the midst of suffering and death**</u>. In Job 13:15 Job said, *"Though he slay me, yet will I trust in him."* NOW – That's strong faith.

The writer of Hebrews goes on to say, in verses 37b & 38b

They wandered about in sheepskins and goatskins; being destitute, afflicted, tormented. ... they wandered in deserts, and in mountains, and in dens and caves of the earth.

The language is vividly descriptive of the savage indignities and severe hardships which men and women of the faith have been willing to endure rather than deny the truth by which they have been liberated.

Like Jesus, they were despised and rejected of men. Their faith cost them everything, but as Jim Elliot put it, **"He is no fool who gives what he cannot keep, to gain what he cannot lose."**

One cannot think of these verses today and not notice the contrast with the so called "health-and-wealth gospel."

For the person whose faith is strong, material comfort mean less, and spiritual values mean more.

The people of God may often be poor and despised, but their faith opens to them riches of spirit, which the world has never known.

Hebrews 11:38a says:

Of whom the world was not worthy: [Emphasis Author's]

The world wasn't worthy of them. They were outlawed as people who were unfit for civilized society; the truth was that civilized society was unfit for them. They might have cried with the Psalmist, as he wrote in Psalms 4:22 *"Yea, for thy sake are we killed all the day long; we are counted as sheep for the slaughter."*

Please, listen to me: Faith in God carries with it <u>no guarantee</u> of <u>comfort</u> in this world; this was no doubt one of the lessons, which the author wished his readers to learn. But it does carry with it great "recompense of reward" in Heaven.

Verses 39-40 are a closing summary:

And these all, having obtained a good report through faith, did not receive the promise, [Emphasis Author's]

This takes us back to the opening statement of the chapter:
Hebrews 11:1-2

Now faith is the substance of things hoped for, the evidence of things not seen. For by it the elders obtained a good testimony.

It is by faith that we please God. Believers, quite often when we see someone suffering we think that God is punishing them, that they must have done something wrong, but note carefully that these all obtained a good testimony.

Are you seeing this? **For some of them God's approval is compatible with physical suffering and persecution.**

The text says they ***"did not receive the promise:"*** **– Question:** What promise is being referred to here?

Prior to the destruction of the Temple in AD 70, "**eternal life**" was a promised future hope, not a present possession. The **promise was eternal life**, resurrection life in the presence of Jesus Christ.

God having provided some better thing for us, that they without us should not be made perfect.

Perfection consists of being resurrected. It's receiving our eternal inheritance.

The Old Covenant Saints did not receive their resurrection until the Old Covenant came to an end and the Church was perfected. Prior to AD 70 and the destruction of the Temple, nobody entered the Presence of God:

Hebrews 10:36-38 gives us a clear understanding of this.

For you have need of endurance, so that after you have done the will of God, you may receive the promise: "For yet a little while, And He who is coming will come and will not tarry. Now the just shall live by faith; But if anyone draws back, My soul has no pleasure in him." [Emphasis Author's]

Now, you might be thinking, "All that martyr stuff was back then, Believers don't suffer today."

I think many folks believe this, because they are so unaware of what is going on in the world outside of North America. Many today are suffering and dying for their faith.

Let me just cite a few of them:

In May 2001 a Hong Kong Christian and businessman was arrested by the Chinese authorities on charges of "assisting an evil cult." Li Guangquiang, 38, was arrested after being caught trying to deliver 16,000 Bibles to a Christian sect called the "Shouters," a house church movement numbering about 500,000. Li was also accused of transporting about 17,000 Bibles in April of that same year.

The Shouters is one among many house church organizations that for decades has refused to join the state-controlled church, therefore labeled as an "evil cult" by the Chinese government. Groups like the Shouters have also been outlawed because of their contacts with western Christians.

Li was arrested in May and indicted in December. Two other Chinese Christians are also being charged in connection with the illegal transporting of the Bibles. The two are Lin Xifu and Yu Zhudi, both who are leaders of the Shouters.

The <u>South China Morning Post</u> (January 8, 2002) reported that President George W. Bush had taken a personal interest in the detention of Li and ordered US diplomats to take up his case. A spokesman for the U.S. Embassy was quoted as saying, "Reports of a crackdown on religious practitioners in China are deeply troubling. We call upon China as a member of the international community to meet international standards on the freedom of religious expression and freedom of conscience."

In court, in the city of Fu Qing, Li was charged with "using an evil cult to damage a law-based society." The reference to an "evil cult" could have resulted in Li receiving the death sentence. He was later released from prison, because of President George W. Bush's intervention.

In another high-profile case in China, house church leader, Gong Shengliang, was arrested and was sentenced to be put to death on January 5, 2002. Gong was granted a reprieve from his death sentence after the case attracted attention from human rights groups and U.S. government officials. According to the news agency, "Compass," Gong had been given a death sentence in a December 18 secret trial in Hubei province on charges of "complicity in rape" and "leading an evil cult." Gong is the leader of the 50,000 members "South China" house church movement.

The following is a summary from excerpts translated and paraphrased from a letter ICC (International Criminal Court) received from 3 Ethiopian Christians describing the horrendous ordeal of torture, terror, and torment they have been through at the hands of an official at the Bremen deportation prison in Jeddah.

The 3 Ethiopians are Baharu Mengistu, Tinsae Gezachew, and Gebeyehu Tefera. The torturous treatment was in retaliation for to a petition sent to the Ethiopian consulate in Jeddah describing their situation in the Bremen deportation prison in Jeddah. The 3 Christians were never charged, but sources say they were arrested due to their Christian faith:

On January 28, 2002, by order of the Bremen Prison Commander Major Bender Sultan Shabani and with no hearing, trial, or process of law, we were illegally subjected to severe punishment and physical abuse.

Being suspended with chains, each of us were flogged 80 times with a flexible metal cable, and also severely kicked and beaten with anything that came into their hands. This was witnessed by over 1,000 deportees.

Our bodies are wounded, swollen, terribly bruised, and with great pain. Baharu's kidney may have been damaged and he is passing blood with his urine. When we reported to the prison hospital for treatment, we were slapped and told to come back after we were dead. It seems as if we were brought to Bremen Deportation Prison to be tortured and tormented to death.

One Ethiopian-Yemeni named Ahmed is the primary instigator of all of this. He is an extortionist who has for a long time been intimidating and threatening Ethiopian Christians working in Jeddah. If they will not pay him blackmail money, he invents serious false charges such as having blasphemed Islam, and reports it to his connections with the Saudi authorities.

Ahmed has been doing some work for the Bremen Prison during this time, and has been continually threatening us, and anyone who comes to visit us. He tells visitors that he will put them in prison also the way he did us. We believe he is also the mastermind behind the delays for our deportation using his connections with prison officials.

A few days before this incident, we sent a petition to the Ethiopian Consulate in Jeddah, with copies to government offices in Addis Ababa, various media sources, and international human rights organizations. In this letter we described our present situation. We have now been imprisoned for 6 months for being Followers of the Christian faith, having never been formally charged with anything.

Finally, about 4 weeks ago, Governor Prince Abdul Majid decided on our deportation after much pressure from several governments and international human rights organizations. By the way, we believe this governor had no knowledge of our recent beating and torture and needs to be informed of this incident. Since then, we have been transferred from the Sharafiah Prison to one deportation facility for a few days, and then to this inhumane deportation cell of the Bremen Prison.

The room we are in is only 11.5 X 30 meters, with at times up to 1,800 men of all nationalities crammed into this tiny space. There is no furniture – no space to lie down except for short naps taken in shifts on the floor. About 80% of the inmates including us have been infected with contagious diseases. Some have AIDS. The toilets are overflowing. The food is not clean. When we complain, we are chained and handcuffed as punishment.

I don't think you could find a greater contrast between the Twenty First Century North American church and the church in the rest of the world than in the area of suffering.

As we study the New Testament church and the church around the world, and examine the attitude and perspective which they have toward persecution, we should be ashamed.

- Why does God allow Christians to suffer?
- What is its purpose in our lives?

I'm sure we could find several reasons why God has His People suffer, but I think the foremost reason is found in the last half of 2 Corinthians verse 9:

2 CORINTHIANS 1:8-9

> *For we do not want you to be ignorant, brethren, of our trouble which came to us in Asia: that we were burdened beyond measure, above strength, so that we despaired even of life. 9 Yes, we had the sentence of death in ourselves, <u>that we should not trust in ourselves but in God who raises the dead.</u> [Emphasis Author's]*

Hear me: It is during the times of suffering and persecution that we learn to trust in God.

What can we do for our brothers and sisters in Christ around the world who are suffering and dying for their faith?

2 Corinthians 1:10-11

> *who delivered us from so great a death, and does deliver us; in whom we trust that He will still deliver us, you also <u>helping together in prayer for us</u>, that thanks may be given by many persons on our behalf for the gift granted to us through many.* [Emphasis Author's]

We can pray for them. If that seems trite to you, then you do not understand the nature of prayer or the power of God.

Hopefully, this message has been a wakeup call for us. We are much too complacent and timid in our faith. We have the Water of Life and the world is dying of thirst.

May we boldly proclaim the glorious gospel of the blessed God. We have the truth, let's pray for the boldness to share it, no matter what the cost. If our boldness brings persecution, it will only cause us to trust more in God and better equip us to minister to others.

As we bring this teaching to a close, remember the following passage of Scripture:

1 Peter 4:12-16 states:

Beloved, do not think it strange concerning the fiery trial which is to try you, as though some strange thing happened to you; but rejoice to the extent that you partake of Christ's sufferings, that when His glory is revealed, you may also be glad with exceeding joy. If you are reproached for the name of Christ, blessed are you, for the Spirit of glory and of God rests upon you. *On their part He is blasphemed, but on your part He is glorified. But let none of you suffer as a murderer, a thief, an evildoer, or as a busybody in other people's matters.* <u>Yet if anyone suffers as a Christian, let him not be ashamed, but let him glorify God in this matter.</u> [Emphasis Author's]

At times we could forget that we are called to suffer reproach for walking with Jesus. And that when this occurs it is actually a huge blessing upon our lives.

We have to be so careful that we have not "bought" into the "love everybody and everything" fruit that we cannot make a true STAND for Jesus.

Yes, we are to love everyone but not the way some people think. At times you have to love people enough to tell them the truth, even when they do not want to hear you.

Remember He is Lord, yes we have been bought with a Price and as such we must Glorify Him who paid the price...

Trust Him Saints, in all of life's circumstances. REMEMBER: Faith pleases God!

Let's check our Understanding of Chapter 10: Faith/Believe

1. What is the key ingredient for us to live a life worthy and justified in the presence of God?

2. What are the 7 key factors the bible reveals about faith and its attributes?

3. Which Scripture talks about faith as triumphant over adversity – victory and accomplishment in spite of trial?

4. What is the other side of Faith that is revealed in Hebrews 11: 35^b-38?

5. What is the Greek word translated "tumpanizo" and what is it's literal meaning?

6. How is the present-day connotation of "martyrs" different from the First Century martyrs who were tortured, not accepting their release, so that they might obtain a better resurrection?

7. Are you able to consider "mockings" because of our faith to be the mildest form of suffering in comparison to those who went before us in the previous generations?

8. Do you believe that if we are not being mocked, sneered at, scoffed at, it is because we are too lax in our ways, too quiet in our talk, or too worldly in our walk? Explain

9. Can you agree with the authors statement "one of the worst tortures was not that of the body but of the conscience; when the torturer would offer the victim opportunity to recant and thus obtain his freedom."? Expound

10. Explain "By faith one lived, and by faith the other died. "

11. What is the hallmark of strong faith?

12. Is there a guarantee of comfort upon earth for those who are of faith? What really does God promise to His faithful Believers?

13. What do you understand by "they did not receive the promise"?

14. Why was it necessary for them to be in hades until the Old Covenant ended in order to receive the promise?

15. What do you believe is the purpose for God allowing us suffer sever persecution even to death?

16. What can we as Christians in North America, not called to suffer such sever persecution due to our faith, called to do?

17. What is your resolve in standing for the Gospel .... The very essence of life that the world is starved of. Are you ready to be reproached for the sake of the gospel?

CHAPTER ELEVEN
FAITH AND PERSECUTION

Please hear me, this message is not designed to give us, any sort of "martyr **or persecution complex**"! No, a thousand times NO! This is to give us as much as possible a balanced understanding of the value of persecution and why it is necessary for us to both understand and accept it. So here we go!

Hebrews 11:35b-40

> Others were tortured, not accepting deliverance, that they might obtain a better resurrection. Still others had trial of mockings and scourgings, yes, and of chains and imprisonment. They were stoned, they were sawn in two, were tempted, were slain with the sword. They wandered about in sheepskins and goatskins, being destitute, afflicted, tormented—of whom the world was not worthy. They wandered in deserts and mountains, in dens and caves of the earth. And all these, having obtained a good testimony through faith, did not receive the promise, God having provided something better for us, that they should not be made perfect apart from us.

Are you familiar with the expression, **"fat, dumb and happy"**? I think that would be an appropriate description of the Twenty-First Century North American Church.

The church in North America has become **fat**—we have so much and appreciate so little. We need the same warning that God gave to Israel as they entered the Promise Land:

Deuteronomy 8:11-14

Beware that you do not forget the LORD your God by not keeping His commandments, His judgments, and His statutes which I command you today, "lest; when you have eaten and are full, and have built beautiful houses and dwell in them; "and when your herds and your flocks multiply, and your silver and your gold are multiplied, and all that you have is multiplied; "when your heart is lifted up, and you forget the LORD your God who brought you out of the land of Egypt, from the house of bondage."

We are **dumb** – the depth of our understanding of God's Word is 3,000 miles wide but only an inch deep.

We have this idea that God wants us all healthy, wealthy, and trouble free. After all, we are North Americans, and we have God's special favour.

We are **happy** – but only as long as things go our way. The idea of being persecuted for the Christian faith sounds outdated like something from the ancient past.

We are comfortable, prosperous, and content in our biblical ignorance, and think we will never have to suffer for our faith.

How does what we see here in North American square with what we read in 2 Timothy 3:12?

2 Timothy 3:12

Yes, and all who desire to <u>live godly</u> in Christ Jesus <u>will suffer persecution</u>. [Emphasis Author's]

Is that true only for the Saints who lived in the transition period, between the Old and New? No! This is a truism for all Saints who live a consistent, godly, Christ-like Christian life.

Hear me: Living righteously in a world filled with evil men will bring persecution. This is why we are so often silent about our faith. We fear the insults, rejection, and persecution that come from a world that hates Christ.

As Christians, we at times are verbally persecuted for our love for Christ. But this is easily avoided by keeping our mouths shut when we're around unbelievers. We know how to blend right in, so as to avoid the slightest persecution. This is very sad and dishonoring to God who wants us to be salt and light to the world in which we live (Matthew 5:13-16).

Because no one likes rejection, we often keep our mouths shut about our faith. Maybe we have even been made to feel like we should cower and hide because of what we believe.

Saints, we need to be willing to suffer for the truth!

Let's be bold in sharing God's truth.

Yes, it will cause persecution, we may lose friends, and we may be called names. But if these things cause us to back down from sharing the truth, we need to be ashamed of ourselves. This is the response we should have:

Matthew 5:11-12

Blessed are you when they revile and persecute you, and say all kinds of evil against you falsely for My sake. Rejoice and be exceedingly glad, for great is your reward in heaven, for so they persecuted the prophets who were before you.

When was the last time you rejoiced when people persecuted you? Oh, we may suffer here and now for what we believe, but we will be rewarded for it in Heaven. BELIEVE THIS!!!

Do we have any idea as to what is going on with Christians in the rest of the world?

Many are suffering and dying for their faith in Christ. This morning I want us to look at the subject of **faith and persecution** in an effort to strengthen and encourage us to be bolder in our faith, and to cause us to be in prayer for our brothers and sisters around the world who are suffering.

When we think of Christians suffering for their faith, we often think of the Saints of the transition period (Pentecost to Holocaust) from AD 30 to AD 70.

However, what I want us to see is that Believers have **ALWAYS suffered for their faith when they lived righteously.**

The Old Testament Saints suffered, the New Testament Saints suffered, and Christians living today still suffer and die for their faith in Jesus Christ.

Let's look at what the Scriptures tell us about the sufferings of faith. Hebrews, chapter 11 is a call to faith. In this chapter we are encouraged to live by faith, trusting God in every situation and circumstance of life:

Hebrews 11:6

But without faith it is impossible to please Him, for he who comes to God must believe that He is, and that He is a rewarder of those who diligently seek Him.

There is just no way our life can be pleasing to God apart from faith. He is pleased with us when we trust Him.

All Believers have faith, but they don't all have the same amount of faith. There are degrees of faith, and we are to always be growing in our faith.

How do we grow in faith? Not by time in service, you don't automatically grow. We grow by increasing our knowledge of God through the study of His Word.

The more we know Him, the more we will trust him. Do you trust people you don't know? Of course not. That is why many Christians find it difficult to trust God; they don't know him very well.

We must study the Bible if we're ever going to grow in faith. But study alone won't do it; we must apply what we know. As we study the Word of God and apply what we learn, we will grow in our faith.

Let's check our Understanding of Chapter 11: Faith And Persecution

1. Do you believe the North American Church is guilty of having the mind set of "Comfort, Prosperity and content in our biblical ignorance and are confident of never having to suffer for our faith" as the author states?

2. According to 2 Timothy 3:12, what can we be assured of as Christians who live a consistent, godly Christ-like life upon this earth?

3. Why is persecution inevitable for Spirit filled Christians who are following Jesus Christ?

4. What type of persecution are we subjected to her in North America and why should we not cower in such situations?

5. What does God's promise in Matthew 5:11-12 tell us?

6. How are we encouraged to live as Christians by Apostle Paul in Hebrews 11?

7. Are you growing in your faith daily? Does your daily routine put God in first place as we profess and allocate time to get to know Him and trust Him?

8. What action plan do you have, to put into practice what you learn on a daily basis?

Chapter Twelve
The Victories of Faith

So, in our last chapter we dealt with **Faith and Persecution** and in this chapter I would like for us to look at the other side – **The Victories Of Faith**!

Hebrews 11:30-35a

By faith the walls of Jericho fell down after they were encircled for seven days. By faith the harlot Rahab did not perish with those who did not believe, when she had received the spies with peace. And what more shall I say? For the time would fail me to tell of Gideon and Barak and Samson and Jephthah, also of David and Samuel and the prophets: who through faith subdued kingdoms, worked righteousness, obtained promises, stopped the mouths of lions, quenched the violence of fire, escaped the edge of the sword, out of weakness were made strong, became valiant in battle, turned to flight the armies of the aliens. Women received their dead raised to life again.

As we look at the 11th chapter of Hebrews, let's keep in mind its context in the book. The theme of the book is found in:

Hebrews 10:23

Let us hold fast the confession of our hope without wavering, for He who promised is faithful.

The very heart of the book is a solemn plea to Jewish Believers not to return to Judaism, thus committing apostasy. He was urgently trying to get them to remain faithful.

This book is a call to endurance, to faithfulness, and maturity in the midst of trials and persecutions:

Hebrews 10:35-39

Therefore, do not cast away your confidence, which has great reward. For you have need of endurance, so that after you have done the will of God, you may receive the promise: "For yet a little while, And He who is coming will come and will not tarry. Now the just shall live by faith; But if anyone draws back, My soul has no pleasure in him." But we are not of those who draw back to perdition, but of those who believe to the saving of the soul.

We're to live by faith, trusting in God in each and every experience of life.

The life of faith is the life of victory.

The writer's design in chapter 11 is to encourage us through the examples of those who by faith were victorious.

We come to the story of the fall of Jericho, which is another example of the victory of faith:

Hebrews 11:29-30

By faith they passed through the Red Sea as by dry land, whereas the Egyptians, attempting to do so, were drowned. <u>*By faith the walls of Jericho fell down*</u> *after they were encircled for seven days.* [Emphasis Author's]

So please understand this:

If you were just reading the NT and did not know what went on for this statement to be made you would absolutely miss the point.

Turn with me to Joshua 5 and let's look at the historical setting:

Joshua 5:6

For the children of Israel walked forty years in the wilderness, till all the people who were men of war, who came out of Egypt, were consumed, because they did not obey the voice of the LORD; to whom the LORD swore that He would not show them the land which the LORD had sworn to their fathers that He would give us, "a land flowing with milk and honey."

Now this account from Joshua tells us why there is such a gap between verse 29 and 30 of Hebrews 11. The generation of Israelites that came out of Egypt would not trust God, and because of their unbelief, they spent 40 years wandering in the wilderness until everyone who was over twenty had died.

Joshua 6:1-5

Now Jericho was securely shut up because of the children of Israel; none went out, and none came in. And the LORD said to Joshua: "See! I have given Jericho into your hand, its king, and the mighty men of valor. "You shall march around the city, all you men of war; you shall go all around the city once. This you shall do six days. "And seven priests shall bear seven trumpets of rams' horns before the ark. But the seventh day you shall march around the city seven times, and the priests shall blow the trumpets. "It shall come to pass, when they make a long blast with the ram's horn, and when you hear the sound of the trumpet, that all the people shall shout with a great shout; then the wall of the city will fall down flat. And the people shall go up every man straight before him."

This was an unusual call for faith; it sure sounded like a strange way to conquer a city.

Their situation: They had just crossed the Jordan River, and by doing so had burned all their bridges. They had nowhere to run, they were now in the enemy's territory, and they had to fight or die. Have you ever found yourself in such a situation? Where you just had no way to retreat! Every bridge to your past has been burned so the only thing that you can do, well one of two things you can do is – move forward or die...

Jericho was a walled city, actually a fortress. It contained an armed garrison filled with experienced warriors.

Jericho had to be defeated before the valleys of Canaan could be occupied. This is one of the cities that frightened the spies, causing them to say, *"The people are greater and taller than we, the cities are great and walled up to heaven".* To their eyes, and minds the city seemed impregnable.

But by faith, they obeyed God. It took a tremendous amount of faith to follow through with this plan.

They could have asked... What – march around the city?

What if the Canaanites shot at them, or dropped rocks on them from the top of the wall? Nothing could seem more foolish than for grown men to march around a strong fortress for seven days on end led by seven priests blowing rams horns.

Joshua 6:10

Now Joshua had commanded the people, saying, "You shall not shout or make any noise with your voice, nor shall a word proceed out of your mouth, until the day I say to you, 'Shout!' Then you shall shout."

QUESTION HERE: WHY WERE THEY TO KEEP SILENT?

Remember, these men were the immediate descendants of the greatest grumblers who ever lived.

Their fathers complained and murmured until God swore in His wrath they should not enter into His rest. (See Exodus 5:1-22, Exodus 14:11-12, Exodus 15:22, Exodus 16:1-4, Exodus 17:1-4, Numbers 11, Numbers 12:1-12, Numbers 14:1-10, Numbers 16, Numbers 20:1-5, Numbers 21:4-5 also 1 Corinthians 10)

How much trouble would have been caused if every man had been left free to express his opinion?

All it takes is just one negative, griping person to get people stirred up.

So then, God was protecting them from themselves by having them to march silent around the wall of Jericho.

Joshua 6:15-16

> *But it came to pass on the seventh day that they rose early, about the dawning of the day, and marched around the city seven times in the same manner. On that day only they marched around the city seven times. And the seventh time it happened, when the priests blew the trumpets, that Joshua said to the people: "Shout, for the LORD has given you the city!"*

Joshua 6:20-21

> *So the people shouted when the priests blew the trumpets. And it happened when the people heard the sound of the trumpet, and the people shouted with a great shout, that the wall fell down flat. Then the people went up into the city, every man straight before him, and they took the city. And they utterly destroyed all that was in the city, both man and woman, young and old, ox and sheep and donkey, with the edge of the sword.*

They obeyed God and He destroyed the city. **Their victory was accomplished by faith, in obedience to the word of the Lord...**

I like what Chrysostom said, "Assuredly the sound of trumpets is unable to cast down stones, though one blow for ten thousand years, but faith can do all things."

The faith of Joshua and the children of Israel serve as a good illustration of the Christian life.

A Christian is never going to live the Christian life without running, sooner or later, into some Jericho, some massive kind of problem.

It is by this same faith that other Jerichos, both large and small, can be overcome.

For the NT Believer this is our reality...

2 Corinthians 10:3-4

> *For though we walk in the flesh, we do not war according to the flesh. For the weapons of our warfare are not carnal but mighty in God for pulling down strongholds,* [Emphasis Author's]

Our warfare is spiritual and so are our weapons.

We all have our Jerichos, and it is by faith that we conquer them.

Did Jericho fall because of the shouting, or trumpets, or marching around it? NO, it fell **by faith;** God told them what to do and they obeyed Him.

Saints, you can't conquer your problem by marching around it, God never told **you** to do this. Many Believers have used this tactic in order to get something from God.

I know of Believers who have marched around land claiming it for God. Please, it was their faith, not their particular actions, that caused Jericho's fall.

By faith the walls of Jericho fell down. *So please hear me: whatever your Jericho is, find a promise from God that is applicable to it, and trust Him for the victory.*

Chapter Twelve: The Victories of Faith

Let's check our Understanding of Chapter 12: The Victories of Faith

1. Where do we find the theme of the book of Hebrews?

2. According to Hebrews 10: 35-39 how are we to enjoy a life of victory?

3. What could have been Apostle Paul's intent when he penned Hebrews 11?

4. Why did God not allow the generation who came out of Egypt to enter the promised land?

5. The situation of the Children of Israel:
They had just crossed the _____ River, and by doing so had _____ all their bridges. They had nowhere to _____, they were now in the _____ territory, and they had to _____ or _____. Have you ever found yourself in such a situation? Where you had just had no way to _____! Every _____ to your _____ has been _____ so the only thing that you can do, well one of two things you can do is _____ _____ or _____.

6. Do you believe the Israelites were oblivious to the circumstances presented, where the Canaanites could harm them from their strong fortresses while they marched around the city for seven days?

7. Why do you believe God choose this unusual method of conquering the City?

8. What happened as a result of their obedience to God?

9. How are we, in the present day, called to conquer our own Jericho situations?

10. Even as we march around our Jericho's what should be the topmost in our minds? That we need to essentially possess in order to have God intervene on our behalf?

CHAPTER THIRTEEN
THE VICTORIES OF FAITH II

IN HEBREWS 11:32-35, (WE'LL LOOK AT VERSE 31 AFTERWARDS – LATER ON) THE author gives us some other examples in which faith has enabled the people of God to be victorious over incredible opposition: Let's look at them...

Hebrews 11:32

*And what more shall I say? "For the time would fail me to tell of Gideon and Barak and Samson and Jephthah (*Jeptah*), also of David and Samuel and the prophets;"* [Emphasis Author's]

The implication of the rhetorical question is that there is no need for further elaboration – "I don't have time to continue to go into detail." These names are no more than a random sampling of the many deserving of mention.

The selection made is rather startling, I would not have chosen these men as an example of faith, but God did.

The writer does not go into detail about what these men did. But if we examine the Old Testament record, we find that each man battled against overwhelming odds so that, humanly speaking, there was little chance of his coming out on top.

For men in such positions, faith in God was not a formality. It meant real trust when the odds seemed stacked against them. They set worthy examples for the readers in their difficult circumstances.

They also show us that faith is not a rarity, which the readers might be unlikely to experience. It has been often found, and can be found today. Let's look at some of the examples the writer uses:

Gideon – We're all probably familiar with the story of Gideon; God took a cowardly, weak man and turned him into a man of faith. Let's revisit that account...

Judges 6:11-12

Now the Angel of the LORD came and sat under the terebinth tree which was in Ophrah, which belonged to Joash the Abiezrite, while his son Gideon threshed wheat in the winepress, in order to hide it from the Midianites. And the Angel of the LORD appeared to him, and said to him, "The LORD is with you, you mighty man of valor!"

This is actually comical, Gideon is hiding as he attempts to thresh wheat, and the Lord calls him a "Mighty man of valor."

Judges 6:13

Gideon said to Him, "O my lord, if the LORD is with us, why then has all this happened to us? And where are all His miracles which our fathers told us about, saying, 'Did not the LORD bring us up from Egypt?' But now the LORD has forsaken us and delivered us into the hands of the Midianites."

He questions God's presence with them. Have you ever done that—doubted God's presence in times of trouble?

Judges 6:14-16

Then the LORD turned to him and said, "Go in this might of yours, and you shall save Israel from the hand of the Midianites. Have I not sent you?" So he said to Him, "O my Lord, how can I save Israel? Indeed my clan is the weakest in Manasseh, and I am the least in my father's house." And the LORD said to him, "Surely I will be with you, and you shall defeat the Midianites as one man."

"Surely I will be with you, and you shall defeat the Midianites as one man" – this is the foundation of his faith, he has God's word, but it took some convincing before Gideon was ready to obey.

Gideon repeatedly asked for confirmatory signs, he was slow to trust God. I can relate to Gideon, can't you?

Through a series of events, God took Gideon from a cowering coward to a man of great faith. With 300 men with no weapons, Gideon went up against 135,000-armed trained warriors. The point should be obvious, **they certainly weren't trusting in themselves,** it was all up to God.

Judges 7:19-22

So Gideon and the hundred men who were with him came to the outpost of the camp at the beginning of the middle watch, just as they had posted the watch; and they blew the trumpets and broke the pitchers that were in their hands. Then the three companies blew the trumpets and broke the pitchers; they held the torches in their left hands and the trumpets in their right hands for blowing; and they cried, "The sword of the LORD and of Gideon!" And every man stood in his place all around the camp; and the whole army ran and cried out and fled. When the three hundred blew the trumpets, the LORD set every man's sword against his companion throughout the whole camp; and the army fled to Beth Acacia, toward Zererah, as far as the border of Abel Meholah, by Tabbath."

This is how you are to live the Christian life, by **faith in God**, and not in yourself. Trust in Him, and let Him fight your battles for you. It took a lot of faith to do what Gideon did, he believed God, and he tackled the impossible. Apart from faith, what he did was stupid.

Barak – we're probably not too familiar with Barak. But according to God, who inspired the writing of Hebrews, he was a man of faith. The story of Barak is in Judges 4.

Barak took 10,000 men along with Prophetess Deborah and attacked and defeated the mighty massive force of Sisera. Practically speaking, there was no way Barak could handle Sisera, but God told Barak, ***"I will deliver him into your hand."*** Barak believed God, and won the battle.

Samson – we're all familiar with him, but we might not of have thought of him as a man of faith, but he was:

Judges 15:14-18

When he came to Lehi, the Philistines came shouting against him. Then the Spirit of the LORD came mightily upon him; and the ropes that were on his arms became like flax that is burned with fire, and his bonds broke loose from his hands. He found a fresh jawbone of a donkey, reached out his hand and took it, and killed a thousand men with it. Then Samson said: "With the jawbone of a donkey, Heaps upon heaps, With the jawbone of a donkey I have slain a thousand men!" And so it was, when he had finished speaking, that he threw the jawbone from his hand, and called that place Ramath Lehi. Then he became very thirsty; so he cried out to the LORD and said, <u>"You have given this great deliverance by the hand of Your servant</u>; and now shall I die of thirst and fall into the hand of the uncircumcised?" [Emphasis Author's]

He knew that his strength was from the Lord. It takes a lot of faith to fight 1,000 men, no matter how strong you are. Samson's conquests illustrate the truth of 1 Samuel 14:6; that God is able to save by many or by few.

Jephthah – this is another man that we are not too familiar with.
Judges 11:1

Now Jephthah the Gileadite was a mighty man of valor, but he was the son of a harlot; and Gilead begot Jephthah.

He was a bastard, yet God placed His Spirit upon him and advanced him to the highest dignity and function among His people and prospered him exceedingly:
Judges 11:9

So Jephthah said to the elders of Gilead, "If you take me back home to fight against the people of Ammon, and the LORD delivers them to me, shall I be your head?"

Jephthah trusted in the Lord. He faced tremendous odds, yet believed God and won the victory.
Judges 11:32-33

So Jephthah advanced toward the people of Ammon to fight against them, and the LORD delivered them into his hands. And he defeated them from Aroer as far as Minnith; twenty cities; and to Abel Keramim, with a very great slaughter. Thus the people of Ammon were subdued before the children of Israel. [Emphasis Author's]

Jephthah, because of a rash vow, he sacrificed his only daughter (Judges 11:30-35,39) …

David – an adulterer and a murderer, and yet used as an example of faith.

David spent his whole life facing incredible odds and trusting God for the victory. David said to Goliath in 1 Samuel 17:46, *"This day will the Lord deliver thee into mine hand."* David's victories were by faith.

As we read through the life of David in the Bible, we see that when he trusted God he was strong, and when he didn't trust God he was filled with fear.

Samuel – He never fought in any wars, but he fought the battle of idolatry and immorality. He had to stand up in the midst of a polluted society and speak for God, and that takes faith.

The Prophets – Samuel and the prophets balance the warriors. To fight for God takes faith, but it also takes faith to speak for Him.

All of these men listed are just men, they weren't perfect, they often failed. They were men of like passions with us, and from that fact we may take comfort. He lists among the faithful:

Gideon, a big coward (it took a lot of convincing to get him to trust God) …

Barak, he wouldn't go into battle unless Deborah went with him (what a man) …

Samson, he married a Philistine – he was so weak as to yield the secret of his strength. In so many ways, Samson was a failure, he was a sinful man, and yet he was an example of faith…

Surely, there is a lesson to learn here. These examples are all real people who were not perfect, but in the midst of their weakness, they trusted God, and as they trusted God, they were made strong. But when they failed to trust God, they were weak.

Hear me today: Strong faith does not await our perfection of character. **Faith is a response to who God is, not what we are.**

It's encouraging to me that God would use these men as examples of faith! It helps me to see that I don't have to be perfect to trust God, but as I learn to trust Him, I'll grow. It also shows me that faith can be strong one minute and weak the next, and the key to strong faith is keeping our eyes on God.

Is faith practical? You bet it is, and the next three verses show us just how practical it can be.

Hebrews 11:33-35 lists the accomplishments of faith, their variety shows how many different situations to which faith can be applied. These Believers overcame every imaginable type of adversity through faith:

Hebrews 11:33

> who through faith subdued kingdoms, worked righteousness, obtained promises, stopped the mouths of lions, [Emphasis Author's]

The Greek word for "subdued" is *katagonizomai*, it means: "to fight down" or "to overcome."

They were victorious, Jeptha, David, Gideon. We too are called to overcome a kingdom, the first being – "the kingdom of self":

Romans 8:13

> For if you live according to the flesh you will die; but if by the Spirit you put to death the deeds of the body, you will live. [Emphasis Author's]

This may often seem like a hopeless task, but we can do it by faith. The Old Testament gives us physical pictures of spiritual realities.

"Wrought righteousness" – literally the Greek means: "they executed justice," it refers to leaders who upheld justice against pressures.

"Obtained promises" – by faith they received what God had promised:

Joshua 21:43

> So the LORD gave to Israel all the land of which He had sworn to give to their fathers, and they took possession of it and dwelt in it. [Emphasis Author's]

"Stopped the mouth of lions" – who do you think this refers to? I believe the answer is found in Daniel 6:10-13

> *Now when Daniel knew that the writing was signed, he went home. And in his upper room, with his windows open toward Jerusalem, he knelt down on his knees three times that day, and prayed and gave thanks before his God, as was his custom since early days. Then these men assembled and found Daniel praying and making supplication before his God. And they went before the king, and spoke concerning the king's decree: "Have you not signed a decree that every man who petitions any god or man within thirty days, except you, O king, shall be cast into the den of lions?" The king answered and said, "The thing is true, according to the law of the Medes and Persians, which does not alter." So they answered and said before the king, "That Daniel, who is one of the captives from Judah, does not show due regard for you, O king, or for the decree that you have signed, but makes his petition three times a day."*

Daniel would not be forced into compromising by the threat of the lions, nor should we be by the mocking words and actions of the world's lions today.

Paul wrote, *"But the Lord stood at my side......and I was delivered out of the mouth of the lion."*

VERSE 34 "QUENCHED THE VIOLENCE OF FIRE."
Daniel 3:13-15

> *Then Nebuchadnezzar, in rage and fury, gave the command to bring Shadrach, Meshach, and Abed-Nego. So they brought these men before the king. Nebuchadnezzar spoke, saying to them, "Is it true, Shadrach, Meshach, and Abed-Nego, that you do not serve my gods or worship the gold image which I have set up? "Now if you are ready at the time you hear the sound of the horn, flute, harp, lyre, and psaltery, in symphony with all kinds of music, and you fall down and worship the image which I have made, good! But if you do not worship, you shall be cast immediately into the midst of a burning fiery furnace. And who is the god who will deliver you from my hands?*

They refused to bow. What would you have done? Notice their faith:
Daniel 3:16-17

Shadrach, Meshach, and Abed-Nego answered and said to the king, "O Nebuchadnezzar, we have no need to answer you in this matter. "If that is the case, our God whom we serve is able to deliver us from the burning fiery furnace, and He will deliver us from your hand, O king."

"Our God whom we serve is able to deliver us" – They knew that their God was **able** to deliver them from the furnace, but they had no means of knowing if He would:
Daniel 3:18

But if not, let it be known to you, O king, that we do not serve your gods, nor will we worship the gold image which you have set up.

"But if not... " – had they received a special revelation that their lives would be spared, it would have called for considerable faith to act upon it in the face of the burning fiery furnace, but to behave as they did without any revelation of the kind called for much greater faith.

The people to whom this epistle was sent might well have a fiery ordeal to face in the near future, but whether life or death was their portion, they could be sure of divine companionship in the midst of it such as the three Hebrews enjoyed.

Let's check our Understanding of Chapter 13: The Victories of Faith II

1. Why do you believe the author of Hebrews decided to mention *Gideon, Barak, Samson, Jephthah, David and Samuel* as examples of men of Faith?^

2. What was Gideon's faith based upon?

3. Do you find yourself asking God for confirmation before you could really trust His word spoken to you? Expound

4. Are you allowing God to fight your battles or are you forging yourself ahead and trying to take control of situations/battles that are too difficult for you?

5. Which Scriptures talk about God's ability to save by many or by few?

6. How did Jephthah (an illegitimate child) become the head of his tribe? What can you glean from this example?

7. Is it possible for people with great Faith and have had experienced many victories in life to slump into situations of fear and doubt? What are some biblical examples?

8. What battles were Samuel called to face? How will this example impact you in your own life today?

9. What does all the examples that were mentioned by Apostle Paul in Hebrews 11:32 have in common? How does this speak to your own life?

10. Strong _____ does not await our _____ of character. Faith is a _____ to who _____ is, not what ___ are.

11. What helps in keeping our Faith strong at all times? Can you think of an example of this the New Testament?

12. The author says that "faith is practical". Do you agree? Explain

13. What are we called to overcome through Faith first and foremost?

14. Explain the many accomplishments of Faith and how it applies to our daily walk with God today?

Chapter Fourteen
The Victories of Faith III

Look at the outcome of their faith:
Daniel 3:28-30

> *Nebuchadnezzar spoke, saying, "Blessed be the God of Shadrach, Meshach, and Abed-Nego, who sent His Angel and delivered His servants <u>who trusted in Him</u>, and they have frustrated the king's word, and yielded their bodies, that they should not serve nor worship any god except their own God! "Therefore I make a decree that any people, nation, or language which speaks anything amiss against the God of Shadrach, Meshach, and Abed-Nego shall be cut in pieces, and their houses shall be made an ash heap; because there is no other God who can deliver like this." Then the king promoted Shadrach, Meshach, and Abed-Nego in the province of Babylon.* [Emphasis Author's]

All because they trusted God. God was exalted, and they were physically preserved and promoted.

"Escaped the edge of the sword" – David escaped the sword of Goliath and Saul, and there are many other examples.

"Out of weakness were made strong" – to everyone who has been mentioned above and who will be mentioned below, this declaration is applicable, for faith is the response of all who are conscious of their own weakness and accordingly look to God for strength. This principle can be seen in the last feat of Samson as he destroyed the temple of Dagon or in David's slaying of Goliath.

The key to the Christian's strength is in maintaining a consciousness of his weakness (2 Corinthians 12:7-10). In our weakness, we look to God's strength.

"Became valiant in fight, turned to flight the armies of the aliens" – there are many, many examples of this in the Scripture. All of the judges cited, in addition to David, put foreign armies to flight (1 Samuel 17:51).

Hebrews 11:35

Women received their dead raised to life again. And others were tortured, not accepting deliverance, that they might obtain a better resurrection.

"Women received their dead raised to life again" – Elijah raised the dead son of the widow of Zarephath (1 Kings 17:17-24). Elisha raised the dead son of the Shunammite woman (2 Kings 4:18-37). The faith of these prophets brought back those children from the dead.

I think that it's clear that the dominant thought in all these examples is triumph over adversity, victory in battle because of faith in God.

The chief reason why Believers experience so little victory in their spiritual lives is because their faith is so little in exercise.

We think we are strong, and that's why we're so weak.

We trust too much in ourselves and our own resources and too little in God.

So now let us look at Hebrews 11:31 – A Harlot's Faith

Hebrews 11:31

By faith the harlot Rahab did not perish with those who did not believe, when she had received the spies with peace.

It is the opinion of the world, as judged by its standards, that Christian faith is an utterly useless, wholly impractical commodity. Look at:

Hebrews 11:1

Now faith is the substance of things hoped for, the evidence of things not seen.

The unbeliever has nothing to hope for, nor a belief in the unseen world. It is only natural that he should view faith as something that is useless, if not indeed detrimental.

For the Believer, however, the faith here defined is a **very practical possession**. It is indispensable in terms of living the Christian life.

The only way that we as Believers can please God is by faith, 11:6; *"without faith it is impossible to please Him."* NOTHING we do pleases God if it's not done by faith.

Faith is trusting God, His Person and His Word. As we learn about God from His Word and put into practice what we know, our faith will grow.

Consider Noah, apart from faith, he never would have built the ark and would not have saved himself and his family from the flood.

Consider Moses, apart from faith, he never would have left Egypt, he would have stayed in the palace and enjoyed the temporal pleasures of Egypt.

Saints, faith is a very **practical commodity**; it enables us to do what we could not otherwise do.

Hebrews 11:31

By faith the harlot Rahab did not perish with those who did not believe, when she had received the spies with peace.

The inclusion of Rahab in this recital of heroic examples of faith is of particular interest.

In the first place, Rahab was a **woman** and is the only woman specifically mentioned by our author in this chapter, apart from Sarah (verse 11), who was introduced in close association with Abraham.

The introduction of Rahab as an independent woman may serve to illustrate to us that though there is a difference between men and women in physical functions and social relationships, when it comes to the sphere of faith, there is neither male nor female.

Secondly, Rahab was a **harlot**. Many commentators try to change the meaning of this word *porne* and say she was a hostess. But there is no justification for that, the Greek word *porne* is always translated in the New Testament as: "harlot" or "whore".

I think the designation "harlot" heightens the grace of God. God is no respecter of persons. How many of us would look at a harlot and think there is no hope for her? God's grace turned this harlot into a true worshiper.

Thirdly, Rahab was a **Gentile**; she didn't belong to the covenant people of God. She is an illustration of the truth of the promise that in the seed of Abraham all the nations of the earth would be blessed. (Genesis 22:18).

Here in this list of great men of faith; men like Enoch and Noah, Abraham and Moses, we find listed a Gentile woman who was a Harlot, a harlot who trusted God and saved herself and her family from judgement.

Turn with me to Joshua 2, and let's look at the historical account.

Joshua 2:1

Now Joshua the son of Nun sent out two men from Acacia Grove to spy secretly, saying, "Go, view the land, especially Jericho." So they went, and came to the house of a harlot named Rahab, and lodged there."

Joshua sends out two spies to search out the city of Jericho. These men would have to swim the Jordan river, get into the city, and assess its strength.

They got into the city and ended up in Rahab's house. They had no idea that there was a Believer in that city and even if they knew, how would they find her. God led them right to her house, they were exactly where God wanted them.

But how many Believers would have had a fit because **they were associating with a woman who was known as a harlot?**

I believe Rahab had become a Believer before those spies ever showed up. Let us prove this:

Joshua 2:9-11

and said to the men: "I know that the LORD has given you the land, that the terror of you has fallen on us, and that all the inhabitants of the land are fainthearted because of you. "For we have heard how the LORD dried up the water of the Red Sea for you when you came out of Egypt, and what you did to the two kings of the Amorites who were on the other side of the Jordan, Sihon and Og, whom you utterly destroyed. "And as soon as we heard these things, our hearts melted; neither did there remain any more courage in anyone because of you, for the LORD your God, He is God in heaven above and on earth beneath."

Rahab had heard about God, and she believed. In Hebrews 11:31 it says that those who perished in Jericho "believed not".

The phrase "believed not" is *apeitheo*, which means: "to be disobedient". It speaks of disbelief manifesting itself in disobedience.

Why is it that Rahab believed and nobody else did? Was she better or smarter than everybody else?

Did Rahab continue to be a harlot after she came to faith? I don't believe that she was a harlot at the time the men went to her house. As we will see, **she had a strong faith, and you cannot have a strong faith and live in sin.**

Dead faith continues to live in sin, but not strong faith. Your faith can only be strong when you're walking in fellowship with God.

Let's see just how strong her faith was:

Joshua 2:2-3

And it was told the king of Jericho, saying, "Behold, men have come here tonight from the children of Israel to search out the country." So the king of Jericho sent to Rahab, saying, "Bring out the men who have come to you, who have entered your house, for they have come to search out all the country."

The spies had been seen; they knew they were in Rahab's house – "*Bring out the men who have come to you, who have entered your house...*" What would you do?

Remember what we saw in:

Joshua 2:9

and said to the men: "I know that the LORD has given you the land, that the terror of you has fallen on us, and that all the inhabitants of the land are fainthearted because of you."

She had only two choices.

1. She could turn the men over, or what else could she do?
2. She had hidden the spies on her roof:

Joshua 2:6

But she had brought them up to the roof and hidden them with the stalks of flax, which she had laid in order on the roof.

Rahab answered the king's delegation by affirming that the Israelite men had come to her, but that she did not report them, because she didn't know where they had come from:
Joshua 2:4-5

Then the woman took the two men and hid them. So she said, "Yes, the men came to me, but I did not know where they were from. "And it happened as the gate was being shut, when it was dark, that the men went out. Where the men went I do not know; pursue them quickly, for you may overtake them."

- **Did she know where they came from? Yes!**
- **Did the men go out the gate? No!**
- **Did she know where they were? Yes!**
- **What she told them, the king's men were a bold-faced lie! Yes it was…**

Was Rahab justified in lying as she did?

- Her action of hiding the spies is commended as an act of faith; it's difficult to understand how, the means by which that action was carried out, "namely lying," could be considered a sin.

James 2:25

Likewise, was not Rahab the harlot also justified by works when she received the messengers and sent them out another way?

The term "justification" has two uses:

1. To declare and treat as righteous.
2. To vindicate, to show or demonstrate as righteous.

Paul uses the first meaning and James uses the second meaning.

Rahab was justified by works, when? When she received and sent out the messengers.

THIS IS WHERE IT BECOMES REALLY TRICKY

Now I do not believe that Christians should ever have to lie to other Christians. However, when the situation arises otherwise then I am not so sure about that. So let us take a look at some of the lies told in Scripture and the reasons behind them:

RAHAB

How what she did demonstrate her faith, as she lied to the king's men about the spies? Yes, **she lied, but in doing so, she risked her life for the spies.**

She risked her life for them because she believed in God, and she believed that God had given them the land. She lied **because** of her faith, and God rewarded her for what she did.

Many people have a problem with this because they hold a position that assumes that lying is always wrong. **Is it always wrong to lie?** If it is, then why was Rahab commended?

OKAY LET'S CHECK THIS OUT

Now you might be thinking, "Doesn't the Bible say it's a sin to lie?"

Proverbs 6:16-17

These six things the LORD hates, Yes, seven are an abomination to Him: A proud look, A lying tongue, hands that shed innocent blood,

Colossians 3:9

Do not lie to one another, since you have put off the old man with his deeds,

Yes, the Bible condemns lying, but it also condemns killing:

Exodus 20:13

You shall not murder.

But is it always wrong to kill?

I have asked a few Believers if they felt it was always wrong to lie. Most responded quickly and confidently, "YES!"

I then asked them if it was always wrong to kill, and they responded quickly and confidently, "NO!" They felt that there were times when killing was justified.

So the question then becomes: it's all right to kill under certain circumstances, but it's never right to lie? Hmmmmm – what do you think?

We don't think it's always wrong to kill, because we believe we should execute criminals. If you say that's all right, you're saying that sometimes it's okay to kill.

How about "self-defense," can you kill someone if they're trying to take your life or the life of a loved one? I think so.

How about the military, is it right for a Christian to be in the military? The purpose of the military is, "deter war and ensure national security and in so doing these officers engage in the act of killing and destroying things", isn't it?

Listen, we know that as a rule killing is wrong, but there are times when it is permitted. I believe that same thing is true with respect to lying.

Now, don't get me wrong: **Lying is wrong**, but under certain circumstances, I believe it's permitted.

Question then: Under what circumstances is it okay to lie?

Well, let's look at some Scriptures:

Exodus 1:15-17

Then the king of Egypt spoke to the Hebrew midwives, of whom the name of one was Shiphrah and the name of the other Puah; and he said, "When you do the duties of a midwife for the Hebrew women, and see them on the birthstools, if it is a son, then you shall kill him; but if it is a daughter, then she shall live." <u>But the midwives feared God, and did not do as the king of Egypt commanded them, but saved the male children alive</u>. [Emphasis Author's]

Verse 17 says, *"... but saved the male children alive."* The NASV says, *"... but let the boys live."* The midwives clearly disobeyed the king, but look what they said:

Exodus 1:18-19

So the king of Egypt called for the midwives and said to them, "Why have you done this thing, and saved the male children alive?" And the midwives said to Pharaoh, "Because the Hebrew women are not like the Egyptian women; for they are lively and give birth before the midwives come to them."

They lied, they said they had nothing to do with it, but verse 17 says that they *"saved the male children alive".*

Exodus 1:20

Therefore God dealt well with the midwives, and the people multiplied and grew very mighty.

Notice carefully what verse 20 says, *"Therefore God dealt well with the midwives..."* God **rewarded** and **blessed** the midwives for their brave action of saving the children. If the midwives didn't do anything, why did God bless them? They clearly lied, but they did so to **save lives.** The king didn't deserve the truth.

In 2 Samuel 17 Jonathan and Ahimaaz were sent to warn David of Absalom's plan to kill him:

2 Samuel 17:17-18

Now Jonathan and Ahimaaz stayed at En Rogel, for they dared not be seen coming into the city; so a female servant would come and tell them, and they would go and tell King David. <u>Nevertheless a lad saw them, and told Absalom</u>. *But both of them went away quickly and came to a man's house in Bahurim, who had a well in his court; and they went down into it.* [Emphasis Author's]

They were spotted, and their errand was reported to Absalom.

2 Samuel 17:19

Then the woman took and spread a covering over the well's mouth, and spread ground grain on it; and the thing was not known.

The men have been hidden.
2 Samuel 17:20

And when Absalom's servants came to the woman at the house, they said, "Where are Ahimaaz and Jonathan?" So the woman said to them, "They have gone over the water brook." And when they had searched and could not find them, they returned to Jerusalem."

She lied, and by doing so, saved the young men's lives.
2 Samuel 17:21-22

Now it came to pass, after they had departed, that they came up out of the well and went and told King David, and said to David, "Arise and cross over the water quickly. For thus has Ahithophel advised against you." So David and all the people who were with him arose and crossed over the Jordan. By morning light not one of them was left who had not gone over the Jordan.

The men warned David and he escaped. The woman's lie saved David. I believe that she was justified in lying; Absalom's servants didn't deserve the truth.
1 Kings 22:20-23

And the LORD said, 'Who will persuade Ahab to go up, that he may fall at Ramoth Gilead?' So one spoke in this manner, and another spoke in that manner. "Then a spirit came forward and stood before the LORD, and said, 'I will persuade him.' "The LORD said to him, 'In what way?' So he said, 'I will go out and be a lying spirit in the mouth of all his prophets.' And the LORD said, 'You shall persuade him, and also prevail. Go out and do so.' "Therefore look! The LORD has put a lying spirit in the mouth of all these prophets of yours, and the LORD has declared disaster against you."

God sends a lying spirit to Ahab, and Ahab is killed in battle. Ahab didn't deserve the truth; he only wanted to hear what was pleasing to him:

2 Thessalonians 2:11

And for this reason God will send them strong delusion, that they should believe the lie,

Do You Agree With This Statement?

We must tell the truth when the truth is due. But don't think that everyone is entitled to the truth.

Do you think it is all right to lie to **preserve life?**

Let me share with you the story of a Dutch woman who endured five years of Nazi occupation during World War 2.

It was the policy of the Germans to arrest young Dutchmen and ship them off to camps or to work projects for the Nazi war effort. This woman hollowed out a hiding place beneath the floorboards to hide her son. In this small cubicle she installed a ventilation fan and stored food provisions in the hiding place.

One day as the Nazis were searching the village for young men, the woman hid her son beneath the floor. Without knocking, the soldiers burst into the house armed with submachine guns. After searching the house, they returned to the living room and stood over the very spot where the son was hidden. A soldier said to the woman, "Are you hiding any boys here?"

What was her moral responsibility? Should she have said, "Yes, there is one under the floor?" I think not! She had a moral right to lie. The Nazis had no right to the truth. She replied, "No, there are no boys here." Thereupon the soldiers began to shoot up the floor, all the while watching the Mother's reaction for any hint of panic. She displayed no outward emotion, while inside she was in stark terror. Finally, the soldiers left. Panic-stricken, the Mother rushed to the hiding place. Her son emerged unhurt. Her deception had saved him.

I don't think we are required to tell robbers where we have hidden our valuables.

We put our lights on a timer when we're not home. Why? To deceive!

Soldiers are not required to tell the enemy where their comrades are positioned.

So, I believe that Truth is to be told to those who are due it.

When the two Israelite spies came to check out Jericho, Rahab received them, hid them, and lied to authorities in order to protect them.

The king of Jericho knew that the spies had visited her, but she placed the Lord above the king believing that if she failed to help the spies, she would be killed along with all the other people of Jericho.

Such was her faith in the Lord that she knew that if she failed to help the spies, it meant certain death. If she helped them, and didn't help the king, it was possible that the king wouldn't find out about it, and she and her father's household would be spared in the upcoming invasion.

Her actions were governed by faith – a desire to be with the Lord and his people. Rahab lied, but her lie was an act of faith, she risked her life for what she believed. **She lied to preserve life.**

Joshua 2:12-13

Now therefore, I beg you, swear to me by the LORD, since I have shown you kindness, that you also will show kindness to my father's house, and give me a true token, "and spare my father, my mother, my brothers, my sisters, and all that they have, and deliver our lives from death."

She believed they would take the city.

Joshua 2:14-24

So the men answered her, "Our lives for yours, if none of you tell this business of ours. And it shall be, when the LORD has given us the land, that we will deal kindly and truly with you." Then she let them down by a rope through the window, for her house was on the city wall; she dwelt on the wall. And she said to them, "Get to the mountain, lest the pursuers meet you. Hide there three days, until the pursuers have returned. Afterward you may go your way." So the men said to her: "We will be blameless of this oath of yours which you have made us swear, "unless, when we come into the land, you bind this line of scarlet cord in the window through which you let us down, and unless you bring your father, your mother, your brothers, and all your father's household to your own home. "So it shall be that whoever goes outside the doors of your house into the street, his blood shall be on his own head, and we will be guiltless. And whoever is with you in the house, his blood shall be on our head if a hand is laid on him. "And if you tell this business of ours, then we will be free from your oath which you made us swear." Then she said, "According to your words, so be it." And she sent them away, and they departed. And she bound the scarlet cord in the window. They departed and went to the mountain, and stayed there three days until the pursuers returned. The pursuers sought them all along the way, but did not find them. So the two men returned, descended from the mountain, and crossed over; and they came to Joshua the son of Nun, and told him all that had befallen them. And they said to Joshua, "Truly the LORD has delivered all the land into our hands, for indeed all the inhabitants of the country are fainthearted because of us."

Rahab's testimony gave them courage.
Her faith was rewarded by God: *"By faith the harlot Rahab <u>perished not</u> with them that believed not"* (Hebrews 11:31).
Joshua 6:21-25

And they utterly destroyed all that was in the city, both man and woman, young and old, ox and sheep and donkey, with the edge of the sword. But Joshua had said to the two men who had spied out the country, "Go into the harlot's house, and from there bring out the woman and all that she has, as you swore to her." And the young men who had been spies went in and brought out Rahab, her father, her mother, her brothers, and all that she had. So they brought out all her relatives and left them outside the camp of Israel. But they burned the city and all that was in it with fire. Only the silver and gold, and the vessels of bronze and iron, they put into the treasury of the house of the LORD. And Joshua spared Rahab the harlot, her father's household, and all that she had. So she dwells in Israel to this day, <u>because she hid the messengers</u> whom Joshua sent to spy out Jericho. [Emphasis Author's]

Rahab believed in the God of Israel, and because of that, she was given eternal life. But had her faith not been strong, she would have died at Jericho. Her strong faith not only saved her from destruction, but it saved her family, also.

God honored this woman for her faith, not only by delivering her from judgement, but also by placing her in the Messianic line. According to Matthew 1, Rahab became the mother of Boaz, who became the husband of Ruth, the great-great-grandmother of David. Rahab, the harlot, moved right into the Messianic line. That's God's Grace.

This is an incredible woman; her faith in God was so strong that she put her life on the line. Is your faith that strong?

This woman didn't have the spiritual advantages we have. She had no Scriptures, no teachers, no fellowship; she lived in a vile pagan city, yet she trusted totally in God.

This remarkable woman of faith stands as a rebuke to us, who have so many spiritual advantages and trust so little in God.

Ok then permit me to ask one more question – what do think that those who are smuggling Bibles into restricted countries do?

Is faith practical? You can't get much more practical than saving your life and the life of your family. May we learn to trust God as much as she did.

Not only that but I believe that when it comes to the brethren the truth must always be told. You should never have to lie to the brethren. However, in the world and in dealing with certain situations you may need to lie in order to preserve life – do you agree with this statement?

This brings us to the end of this book and it is my prayer that you were able to receive life from it. Kingdom Blessings!

Let's check our Understanding of Chapter 14: The Victories of Faith III

1. How was Hananiah, Mishael & Azariah spared from being burned in the fiery furnace into which they were thrown?

2. What made David escape the swords of both Goliath and Saul?

3. For _____ (iafht) is the _____ (proenses) of all who are _____ (ncsociosu) of their own weakness and accordingly _____ (loko) to _____ for _____ (nstgreth).

4. What are some of the biblical examples where you see the above principle in operation?

5. According to 2 Corinthians 12:7-10 what is the Key to the Christian's strength?

6. Do you agree with the author's statement "The chief reason why Believers experience so little victory in their spiritual lives is because their faith is so little in exercise." Explain.

7. Expound on the idea that faith, as defined in Hebrews 11:1, is viewed as something useless or detrimental by the unbeliever and yet is something indispensable for a Christian.

8. In this context how will you define Faith?

9. How can we grow in our faith? Explain with biblical examples

10. What is the significance of Rehab being introduced to us by Apostle Paul as an independent woman of faith?

11. Which Scriptures speak to the fact that Rehab was already a believer of God even before the spies entered her house?

12. What is the Greek word translated "believed not" in Hebrews 11:31? What is its meaning? How does it corroborate with those who were destroyed in Jericho?

13. Do you agree that strong faith is only possible when in fellowship with God and therefore it is not possible for someone to continue to live in sin and have strong faith?

14. Do you agree with the author on the subject of lying ... that in certain circumstances it is permissible? Explain.

15. Why do you believe Rahab's was rewarded by God?

OTHER EXCITING TITLES
By Michael Scantlebury

UNDERSTANDING THE REVELATION

As we embark on this study, there are certain things that we need to first establish. Here are five things that I believe the book of Revelation is about:

1. Revelation is the most Biblical book in the Bible.
2. Revelation has a system of symbolism.
3. Revelation is a prophecy about imminent events – events that were about to break loose on the world of the First Century.
4. Revelation is a worship service.
5. Revelation is a book about dominion.

Also, we have to study The Revelation as a part of the entirety of Scripture and not as a separate book on its own. It ties in beautifully with the rest of the Bible and Israel's journey. So, as we study the prophecy within this book, we will see how it ties in with Jesus' prophecy recorded in Matthew 24 and many of the words spoken directly to the tribes of Israel. It was a powerful and very relevant book for the First Century Church and gives us today a clear picture of God's way of dealing with

His people. When approached from this point of view, fresh realms of understanding will herald some fresh and powerful truths for us today.

Also, we need to bear in mind that the Bible is a record of Two Covenants; the Old Covenant which had a shelf life and was destined to come to an end. And then we have the New Covenant which is eternal and as such will never end. It has been eternally established by our King and Lord, Jesus the Christ. We need to add to this the understanding that the entire cannon of Scripture was written prior to AD 70.

ARE WE LIVING IN THE END TIMES OR THE LAST DAYS?

Whenever we hear this term "end-times or last-days" it conjures up all kinds of images in our minds: from the universe blowing up with the largest flames you could ever imagine! And that it would usher in a new heaven and a new earth. We also have presupposed in the body of Christ that before all of this would indeed occur, the righteous would be raptured away and then the world would be left a massive fire of destruction.

When you hear Christians mention the 'last days,' many just assume it's referring to the end of time and of the world. But the attentive Bible student asks, 'last days of what?' It seems obvious to me that the text is referring to the end of the Old Covenant-Temple aeon/age. When you read the New Testament through these lenses, all I can say is WOW! It makes a significant difference, when you read the Scriptures with the realization that the Bible was written FOR you and not TO you.

We need to also understand that "time of the end" and "end of time" are not one and the same thing. The Bible teaches about the "time of the end" but there is nothing taught about an "end of time."

FATHERS AND SONS – AN UNVEILING

As we embark upon this study, there is something that I would like for us to first understand, and it is this: God the Father is the ultimate Father. There has never been anyone like Him, nor is there currently anyone like Him, nor will there ever be anyone like Him. He is in a class all by Himself.

Another thing that we need to understand moving forward is this: Respect produced by force and domination is not respect but fear.

Also, when we speak of sons, we are not only referring to the male gender, but we are speaking of **a new class in God**. Those that have been washed by the Blood of Jesus and have entered the New Covenant with Him. Notice that in the Scriptures, it never states "Sons and Daughters of God."

John 1:12 states

But as many as received him, he gave them power to be made the sons of God, to them that believe in his name. ...

As such, I do believe that women can also be Apostles and in a broader scope, they qualify to "father" should that mantle be upon them.

HEAVEN & EARTH A BIBLICAL UNDERSTANDING

Whenever we today in this 21st Century read about heaven and earth in the Scriptures we need to be careful as to exactly what is being referred to. And here are some reasons as to why this must be.

1. The original Bible was not written in our modern English, which is a far different language than Hebrew and Greek the original languages of the Holy Scriptures. Hence the reason for us to become avid students of the Word of God.

2. We, living today are not the original recipients of Scripture and as such we need to understand what the original recipients understood when they first received that Word.
3. We must be willing to let the Bible interpret itself and not hang on to our theories for the Scriptures.
4. That the Bible speaks of at least four Heavens and three earths. And as such we need to dig deep into the Word of God and find them and apply this understanding in our study.

Remember what the Scriptures say in Proverbs 25:2 *It is the glory of God to conceal the word, and the glory of kings to search out the speech.*

With that said let us now take a deeper dive and journey into the Word of God with the intention of extracting much needed revelation concerning these Heavens and Earths.

MY PONDERINGS

In this book before you the author has been engaged in pondering several subjects and as such, decided to put his thoughts in a book. As you read through these pages may the Lord use his thoughts to both inspire and bless you. Here are some of the subjects he has been pondering, with each one making up a chapter of this book:

My Ponderings on The Kingdom of God
My Ponderings on The Church
My Ponderings on Innovation
My Ponderings on Wisdom and The Power of Vision
My Ponderings on Navigating Seasons
My Ponderings on Breakthroughs
My Ponderings on Unity
My Ponderings on The Many Comings of Jesus
My Ponderings on Eschatology
My Ponderings on Jesus the First Fruit of the Dead
My Ponderings on Understanding the Times
My Ponderings on Understanding the New Covenant
My Ponderings on Gold

Other Exciting Titles

UNDERSTANDING THE KINGDOM OF GOD AND THE CHURCH OF JESUS CHRIST

"This book is a game changer and will teach you what it means to be part of This Kingdom."

> Pastor Marilyn Bailey—Teleios Church,
> Johannesburg,
> South Africa

"There is perhaps no greater time to revisit the spiritual and practical understanding of the kingdom of God than right now.

Apostle Scantlebury addresses and corrects, common misconceptions, explains the contrasts in the Kingdom of God and the kingdom of darkness, properly aligns the Kingdom and the Church, and propels us toward a holistic understanding of Kingdom life in the earth.

With great patience and clear articulation, Apostle Scantlebury lays out a compelling case for the people of God to give priority to understanding and walking in the principles of the Kingdom of God in life and ministry.

Do yourself a favour; set aside some time to read through and study this transformative volume. You will be challenged, changed, and equipped to be a proper representative of the kingdom of God."

> Apostle Eric L. Warren—Eric Warren Ministries
> Charlotte, North Carolina, USA

ESCHATOLOGY – A BIBLICAL VIEW

If you were a time traveler and traveled back to the time of say Abraham Lincoln and told him you were from the future in 21st century. What if he asked you how people communicated in the 21st century, and now you had to try and explain say how an email works. How would you explain it?

Would you use something he would be familiar with to describe it? Perhaps you would tell him that in the future postmen would ride horses at 500 mile per hour. Or you might tell him you could deliver a message by train from New York to LA in less than one day. You're trying to find a way to communicate how "fast" an email really is. But you're trying to do in a way that wouldn't totally blow his mind.

That's kind of the conundrum we have when trying to understand difficult verses in the Bible, especially in themes like eschatology. The prophetic writers of Scripture had to convey God's mysteries in language that their readers would understand.

Fast forward now 2-3,000 years later, and we are reading these prophetic Scriptures through a 21st century lens, and sometimes coming up with all kinds of weird speculative interpretations because we didn't understand what those Scriptures would have meant to a first century Believer, or a Jew living in the time of the OT Prophets.

The book before you plan to delve deeper into this and much more as it seeks to present you with a sensible view of eschatology.

THE RESTORATION OF ZION

When you hear the word Zion, what comes to mind? As Christians, we've sung the choruses and the hymns about Zion or Mount Zion, but do we fully understand just what we're singing about? Do we know what it is? The Bible promises the full restoration of Zion, and if we don't fully know what Zion is, what then do we anticipate in terms of its restoration?

The greatest hindrance to accurate interpretation and application of Scripture is a futuristic view of Scripture. This futuristic view continues to rob the Believer of experiencing God in His fullness in the here and now.

In this book, we will uncover within the Scriptures exactly what Zion actually represents to the New Testament Believer. So lay down any preconceived ideas you may have, delve into the pages of this book, and let it speak truth to you.

AS IT WAS IN THE BEGINNING SO SHALL IT BE...

Have you ever wondered about life and all of its intricacies? Why are we here on planet earth? What is out there in deep dark space? Who created it all in its majesty and wonder with the brilliancy of everything that surrounds us?

Since time began, man has tried to explain things regarding the known world. One forward thinker put forth a theory that the world was flat. That was refuted by more research. Study and research and pondering some more have revealed some truth about our world but not all the questions are yet answered.

While many of us as Christians enjoy documentaries on the pondering of the many ways we may have "gotten here" beginning with the theory of alien transports dropping us off, to the idea of a cosmic slime pit which one day came to life, so truly the only authority we have as born-again followers of Jesus Christ is the book of Genesis, the very first book of the Holy Scriptures, which simply states: "In the beginning God created the heavens and the earth." Genesis 1:1

We will broach the answers to these and other questions only God's inspired word, the Holy Bible will answer the many questions at hand.

We will begin our journey into the heart and mind of this incredible Creator to learn the reason and purpose for our existence. And as we take that incredible journey, we would seek to come to terms with the revealed, eventual outcome of our existence and life upon planet earth.

STUDY GUIDE – DANIEL IN BABYLON

This is an exciting study into the present truth lifestyle illustrated through the lives of Daniel and his friends. Whether you'll be meeting with others in a group or going through this book on your own, you've made an excellent decision by choosing to read **DANIEL in Babylon** and studying it in-depth with this guide.

This is a seminal study with strong Apostolic messaging, yet its flowing style allows for easy assimilation of biblical truths, and provides accurate insights for the cerebral Believer, who like Daniel and his companions, are usually the target of the world system. In this book various methodologies are outlined through which, spiritual Babylon seeks to entice the brightest and best of every Godly generation, to acculturize, rob of spiritual identity and manipulate to promote world kingdom end.

PRINCIPLES FOR VICTORIOUS LIVING: VOL II
The initial purpose of the five-fold ministry is for the perfecting or maturing of the Saints, which leads to its next intention, which is the real work of the ministry of Jesus Christ, reconciling the world back to the Father. This book lends itself to help in the maturing of the Saints. It adds insight and strategies that help in achieving exponential personal growth preparing one for the real work of the ministry. This is a volume of information and revelation needed in such a time as this, when maturity and focus are the needed key components that bring us an overcoming victory in this realm and advance the Kingdom of God.

PRINCIPLES FOR VICTORIOUS LIVING: VOL I
The information contained herein is well balanced with a spiritual maturity that keenly stems from wisdom and revelation in the knowledge of Christ. This is the anointing of an Apostle, and the truths that our brother shares will certainly cause you to excel in the Kingdom of God long before this life is over when later we enter the eternals. There's so much to experience today in this life, and Michael extracts so much from the Word of God to facilitate that. His insight of revelation and ability to interpret and articulate what his spirit receives from the Lord are powerful.

Other Exciting Titles

PRESENT TRUTH LIFESTYLE – DANIEL IN BABYLON

This is a seminal study with strong Apostolic messaging, yet its flowing style allows for easy assimilation of biblical truths, and provides accurate insights for the cerebral Believer, who like Daniel and his companions, are usually the target of the world system. In this book various methodologies are outlined through which, spiritual Babylon seeks to entice the brightest and best of every Godly generation, to acculturize, rob of spiritual identity and manipulate to promote world kingdom end.

But thanks be to God, there is still a generation in the earth spiritually alert enough to operate within the world system, yet deploy their talents and giftings to bring honour and glory to God. Those with the Daniel mindset will decode dreams and visions and interpret judgements written on the kingdoms of this world in this season.

ESTHER PRESENT TRUTH CHURCH

In a season where the Church co-exists harmoniously with truth and error, this book provides us with a precision tool and well-calibrated instrument of change that is able to fine-tune the global Body of Christ.

The Book of Esther is rich with revelation that is still valid and applicable for the day in which we live. Hidden within its pages is a powerful "present truth" message. The lives of the people involved and the conditions that are seen have spiritual parallels for the Church. Our destiny as the Body of Christ is revealed. The preparations and conditions we must attain to are all similar.

THE FORTRESS CHURCH

According to Webster's English Dictionary "fortress" is defined as: a fortified place: stronghold, *especially*: A large and permanent fortification sometimes including a town. A place that is protected against attack. This book seeks to describe what is a "Fortress Church". We would be looking into the dynamics of this Church as described in Jacob's vision in Genesis Chapter 28, also as described by the Prophet Isaiah, in Isaiah Chapter 2 and as the one detailed in a Psalm of the sons of Korah in Psalms Chapter 48. We would also be looking at a working model of this type of church as found at Antioch in the Book of Acts. Finally we would be exploring The Church at Ephesus, where the Apostle Paul by the Holy Spirit revealed some powerful descriptions of The Church.

CALLED TO BE AN APOSTLE

This autobiography spans fifty-two years of my life on the earth thus far and I have the hope of living several more... Our home was always packed with young people and we did enjoy times of really wonderful fellowship! Although we were experiencing these wonderful times of fellowship my appetite and desire to grow in the things of God continued unabated. I continued to read anything and everything that I could put my hands on that would strengthen my life. I began reading Wigglesworth, Moody, Finney, Idahosa, Lake, and the list went on and on! But the more I read the more this question burned in my heart–"*why is it that every time we hear/read about a move of God, it is always miles away and in another country? Why can't I experience some of the things that I am reading about?*" Little did I know the Lord would answer that desire!

LEAVENED REVEALED

The Bible has a lot to say about *leaven* and its effects upon the Believer. Leaven as an ingredient gives a false sense of growth. In the New Testament there are at least six types of *leaven* spoken about and we will be exploring them in detail, in order to ensure that our lives are completely free of the first five, and completely influenced by the sixth! These types of leaven include the following: The leaven of the Pharisees; The leaven of the Sadducees; The leaven of the Galatians; The leaven of Herod; The leaven of the Corinthians. However, the Leaven of the Kingdom of God is the only type of leaven that has the power and capacity to bring about true growth and lasting change to our lives.

I WILL BUILD MY CHURCH — JESUS CHRIST

"For we are his *masterpiece*, created in Christ Jesus for good works that God prepared long ago to be our way of life." Ephesians 2:10

What a powerful picture of The Church of Jesus Christ-His Masterpiece! Reference to a *masterpiece* lends to the idea that there are other pieces and among them all, this particular one stands head and shoulders above the rest! This is so true when it comes to The Church that Jesus Christ is building; when you place it alongside everything else that God has created, The Church is by far His Masterpiece!

JESUS CHRIST THE APOSTLE AND HIGH PRIEST OF OUR PROFESSION

There is a dimension to the apostolic nature of Jesus Christ that I would like to capture in His one-on-one encounters with several people during the time He walked the face of the earth and functioned as Apostle. In this book we will explore several significant encounters that Jesus Christ had with different people where valuable principles and insight can be gleaned. They are designed to change your life.

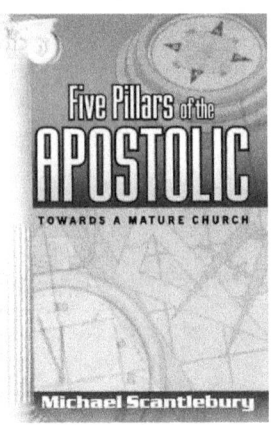

FIVE PILLARS OF THE APOSTOLIC

It has become very evident that a new day has dawned in the earth, as the Lord restores the foundational ministry of the Apostle back to His Church. This book will give you a clear and concise understanding of what the Holy Spirit is doing in The Church today.

APOSTOLIC PURITY

In every dispensation, in every move of God's Holy Spirit to bring restoration and reformation to His Church, righteousness, holiness and purity has always been of utmost importance to the Lord. This book will challenge your to walk pure as you seek to fulfil God's Will for your life and ministry.

GOD'S NATURE EXPRESSED THROUGH HIS NAMES

How awesome it would be when we encounter God's Nature through the varied expressions of His Names. His Names give us reference and guidance as to how He works towards and in us as His people–and by extension to society! As a matter of fact it adds a whole new meaning to how you draw near to Him; and by this you can now begin to know His Ways because you have come into relationship with His Nature.

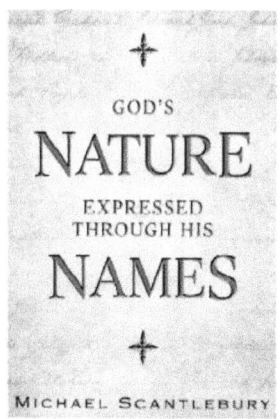

INTERNAL REFORMATION

Internal Reformation is multifaceted. It is an ecclesiology laying out the blue print of The Church Jesus Christ is building in today's world. At the same time it is a manual laying out the modus operandi of how Believers are called to function as dynamic, militant over-comers who are powerful because they carry internally the very character and DNA of Jesus Christ.

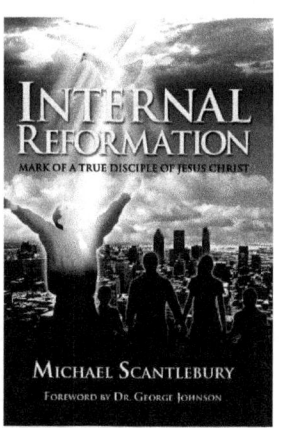

KINGDOM ADVANCING PRAYER VOL I

The Church of Jesus Christ is stronger and much more determined and equipped than she has ever been, and strong, aggressive, powerful, Spirit-Filled, Kingdom-centred prayers are being lifted in every nation in the earth. This kind of prayer is released from the heart of Father God into the hearts of His people, as we seek for His Glory to cover the earth as the waters cover the sea.

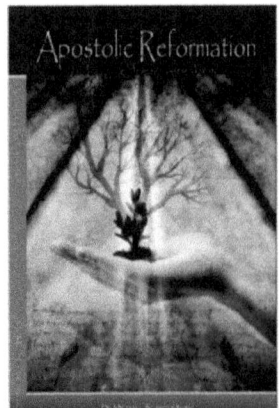

APOSTOLIC REFORMATION

If the axe is dull, And one does not sharpen the edge, Then he must use more strength; But wisdom brings success." (Ecclesiastes 10:10) For centuries The Church of Jesus Christ has been using quite a bit of strength while working with a dull axe (sword, Word of God, revelation), in trying to get the job done. This has been largely due to the fact that she has been functioning without Apostles, the ones who have been graced and anointed by the Lord, with the ability to sharpen.

KINGDOM ADVANCING PRAYER VOL II

Prayer is calling for the Bridegroom's return, and for the Bride to be made ready. Prayers are storming the heavens and binding the "strong men" declaring and decreeing God's Kingdom rule in every jurisdiction. This is what we call Kingdom Advancing Prayer. What a *Glorious Day* to be *Alive* and to be in the *Will* and *Plan of Father God*! Hallelujah!

KINGDOM ADVANCING PRAYER VOLUME III

One of the keys to the amazing rise to greater functionality of The Church is the clear understanding of what we call Kingdom Advancing Prayer. This kind of prayer reaches into the very core of the demonic stronghold and destroys demonic kings and princes and establishes the Kingdom and Purpose of the Lord. This is the kind of prayer that Jesus Christ engaged in, to bring to pass the will of His Father while He was upon planet earth.

IDENTIFYING AND DEFEATING THE JEZEBEL SPIRIT

I declare to you with the greatest of conviction that we are living in the days when Malachi 4:5-6 is being fulfilled. Elijah in his day had to confront and deal with a false spiritual order and government that was established and set up by an evil woman called Jezebel and her spineless husband called Ahab. This spirit is still active in the earth and in The Church; however the Lord is restoring His holy Apostles and Prophets to identify and destroy this spirit as recorded in Revelation 2:18-23.